POWERING UP PERFORMANCE MANAGEMENT

To
Dink and Bill Bunton – two very special people

Peter

POWERING UP PERFORMANCE MANAGEMENT

An integrated approach to getting the best from your people

Richard Hale and Peter Whitlam

Gower

Published by
Gower Publishing Limited
Gower House
Croft Road
Aldershot
Hampshire GU11 3HR
England

Gower
131 Main Street
Burlington
Vermont 05401
USA

Richard Hale and Peter Whitlam have asserted their right under the Copyright, Design and Patents Act 1988 to be identified as the authors of this work.

British Library Cataloguing in Publication Data

Hale, Richard, 1960–
  Powering up performance management : an integrated approach
  to getting the best from your people
  1. Performance   2. Employees – Rating of
  I. Title   II. Whitlam, Peter, 1949–
  658.3'125

  ISBN 0 566 08189 X

Library of Congress Cataloging-in-Publication Data

Hale, Richard 1960–
    Powering up performance management : an integrated approach to getting the best from
  your people/Richard Hale and Peter Whitlam.
      p. cm
    Includes index.
    ISBN 0–566–08189–X (hardback)
    1. Employee motivation.   2. Performance standards.   3. Organizational effectiveness.   I.
  Whitlam, Peter, 1949–   II. Title.

  HF5549.5.M63 H34 2000
  658.3'14–dc21   99-046261

Typeset in Ehrhardt by IML Typographers, Chester and printed
in Great Britain by The University Press, Cambridge.

Contents

List of figures

Acknowledgements

We would like to thank the following people and organizations for their support in contributing to our work in the field of performance management:

Paul Lomas, Ulf Larsen, Estelle Rivals and Paul Wesley at Allied Domecq Spirits and Wine
Roland Triffaux and Grace Hughes at Xilinx
Dr Alan Mumford for his support in Richard Hale's mentoring research
Coca-Cola
Scottish Hydro-Electric
Lotus Development
International Management Centres

Introduction

The rationale for choosing to write this book was based on our growing disenchantment with the way in which many organizations, often leaders in their field, fail to maximize returns from what they often describe as their greatest asset – their people. Associated with this observation was the recognition that, at an individual level, many people do not achieve to the best of their ability. It has been estimated that most human beings achieve less than 1 per cent of their actual potential. Admittedly, the individual has something to answer for here, but it is sadly often the case that the organization, which could provide fertile territory for personal growth, is actually an inhibitor.

This book provides insights and practical ideas on how you can 'power up' your team's or organization's performance through the development of its people. It is ideally suited for 'organizational architects' – those who have responsibility for shaping their team or organization, its processes, values and behaviours. You may be operating from a corporate perspective or be responsible for the management of human resources in your organization and looking for a resource to help in developing an effective performance management strategy. Alternatively, you may have responsibility for management or organizational development, in which case the book will provide support by way of the integrated model and associated tools and techniques.

The book presents a holistic view of the management of performance. It is suggested that effective performance management commences with making the right decision at the selection stage and continues through to target setting, coaching performance appraisal, and even mentoring. We believe that the most effective organizations in terms of performance management in the future will be those that take all of these stages of the process seriously. This will be one of the key routes through to the achievement of broader organizational goals in pursuit of the vision.

Our experiences and observations of many organizations lead us to the conclusion that performance management tends to focus on the hard measurable business outputs of the organization. This focus ignores the important issue of how such outputs – say, sales or production – will be achieved. We aim to address this imbalance within this text because we believe that concentrating on 'hard' measures alone generates organizational discord and, at times, dysfunctional behaviour. For example, in many organizations targets are set primarily along traditional business lines where it is stated that 'the individual will achieve x by y'. As suggested, this approach only tackles part of the performance management problem. It is our contention that, in order to achieve sustained business performance, it is equally necessary to recognize and focus on what we describe as the 'inputs' – the skills or how people achieve the outputs.

So what are the consequences of this overemphasis on the 'hard' measurable targets for an organization? Below are some of the symptoms we have seen in organizations where performance management processes concentrated almost exclusively on the 'what', thereby ignoring the 'how':

- Individuals hold different definitions of successful performance.
- There is inconsistency in selection, based primarily on the fact that the organization is unclear about what it is looking for.
- People are assessed against different criteria and perceptions of what good performance looks like.
- There is a failure in understanding which skills can be developed and which are innate.
- Underperformance is not addressed, largely because managers are unable to describe good performance in behavioural terms.
- Efforts are misdirected and people focus on the wrong or destructive activities.
- Training and development fails to meet the real individual and organizational needs.
- There is an overemphasis on courses and programmes rather than coaching and facilitating learning in the work environment.

The picture is not just one of doom and gloom, though. We sense a changing mood, with the more enlightened organizations taking care to define successful performance clearly. These organizations are recognizing that the idea of 'people as our most important asset' is more than just a platitude. They demonstrate that they mean it by treating the management of individual performance with the same degree of rigour as they have traditionally treated their less human assets: they purchase with care, they invest, review, measure and nurture.

In this book we advocate the use of what we describe as behavioural competencies, or specifically stated definitions of what people are expected to do. This means initially taking quite an analytical approach in describing successful performance and then using this analysis to inform all aspects of performance management. We advocate the use of such descriptions throughout the employee life cycle – at selection, when determining development needs and when setting objectives. This holistic focus on inputs, or the 'how' underpins this book and, in our experience, effective performance management.

The book is intended to challenge your thinking by raising such questions as: 'How do we measure up in our organization?', ' What do I need to do in order to enhance my organisation's approach to performance management?' and 'How effective am I in managing the performance of my own team?'

Structure and style of the book

Throughout the book we draw on a number of case studies based on our own experience in a number of organizations that we believe are operating at the leading edge of human resource management. We show, for instance, how Coca-Cola has used behavioural technology as a way of building and managing high performance against a backdrop of a rapidly changing business environment. We show how Allied Domecq has implemented a worldwide coaching and mentoring programme as a key component of its broader performance management strategy. We draw on our experience in a range of business sectors and show how utility organizations, such as Scottish Hydro-Electric, have given performance and development of people a higher profile. These case studies give an international flavour to the book and demonstrate that the principles we advocate are portable across all sectors and organizational levels. We urge you to enquire and explore the content of this book with an open mind. You should think about how the ideas presented can be practically adapted and incorporated into your organization's approach to performance management. Opposite to this mindset is an approach which is captured by the phrase 'terminal uniqueness'. This describes organizations or teams within organizations whose membership expresses views such as 'yes that sounds great but it can't work here because we are different'. Such closed-mind thinking is clearly the root cause of organizational stagnation. By stating this we do not mean to insult the reader, only to endorse the point made clearly by Argyris and Schon (1996) in their seminal text on organizational learning when they identified that there are a number of human and political dynamics that surface in the organizational context and conspire to inhibit openness to learning and change.

Each chapter commences with a description of its specific objectives. These will provide understanding regarding the content of the chapter. Context and relevant theory is provided along with case studies that illuminate organizational practices. Each chapter concludes with a section entitled 'Pause for Thought', which helps you consider and contrast aspects of your own organization's approach in relation to the performance management issue described within the chapter.

As well as drawing on our own consultancy experience in working with clients referenced in the case studies, we draw heavily on our own academically validated action research. For example, Chapter 6, which covers the subject of mentoring as a route to organizational learning, was written while conducting doctoral level research into the subject, where there was a requirement to search the literature and understand organizational best practice.

We now introduce you to the book by providing you with an outline of the individual chpaters of this text showing how they build a picture of performance management which commences with understanding the role of the employee or organizational member through to recruitment, appraisal, objective setting, coaching and mentoring,

Chapter 1: The problem of measurement

The underlying theme behind this book is that 'What gets measured gets done'. We begin this chapter by looking at the emergence of performance management as a concept and outline some of the historical developments in this area. Some of the more recent research into the challenges facing organizations when attempting to establish performance management strategies are discussed, and the overall importance of measurement is stressed. We explain a key model that suggests that any outputs achieved by an individual are simply the composite of a number of behaviours or skills that are deployed. The need to reach behind the outputs in order to identify the behaviours required to achieve the result is a key concept.

Although we advocate a holistic approach to the management of performance, we go on to explore a model of performance management which is essentially analytical, breaking down the employment cycle into stages as a means of structuring the book. At each of these stages performance management can be 'brought to life' not just for the individual but for all organizational members. The basic model is shown in Figure I.1.

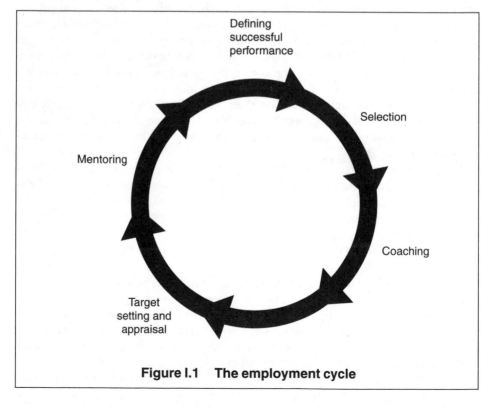

Figure I.1   The employment cycle

You will probably be familiar with certain aspects of this model, depending on your experience of human resource management. However a number of questions can occur at an *individual level*:

- To what extent do you, as an individual, practise effective performance management with those for whom you are responsible?
- Do you define success clearly?
- Do you recruit against an agreed format?
- Do you set clear performance objectives, including expectations in terms of behaviours?
- Do you use a consistent approach to reviewing performance and identifying development needs?
- Do you coach effectively in order to improve performance in the current role?
- Do your people have an opportunity to develop effective mentoring relationships?

Equally, there are a number of questions to consider at an *organizational level*:

- To what extent does your organization integrate these key stages through systems and practice?
- Is effective performance management institutionalized in the organization?
- Is there a culture which encourages good practice in terms of the management and development of people?
- At an organizational level, what can you do to help your organization move towards a better integration of the key dimensions of performance management?

We describe best practice at each stage of the performance management cycle, allowing comparison and identification of actions that you can take to help power up your own, and your organization's, approach to performance management. The subsequent chapters of the book follow the sequence of the model, building a picture of the the 'nuts and bolts' of effective performance management at the individual level. It is important to stress that there are no easy short-cuts in our experience, no simple single action or system that can be introduced resulting in effective performance management – you should question yourself and your organization with respect to each stage of the performance management cycle as described.

Chapter 2: Defining successful performance

Defining success is seen as the essential first step in managing performance. Without a systematic approach to defining the behaviours initially required by the role-holder how can you and your organization begin to manage performance and develop individual performance?

This chapter considers a number of techniques and tools for bringing some robustness to defining the skills and behaviour required for success in a role.

These approaches include the use and application of structured interviewing, embracing such techniques as critical incident analysis, diary techniques and repertory grid. We go on to show how a Skills Analysis Questionnaire can be used as a practical tool for quickly defining the characteristics required for success in any given job. An actual example of a Skills Analysis Questionnaire is provided in Appendix 1. We describe the output from the use of such processes as the behavioural profile for a role or job.

By using the tools described in this chapter you should be able to assess your organization's approach to role definition and be able to recommend, or implement, a more focused and defensible approach to defining what are often assumed to be the intangibles of human behaviour.

Chapter 3: Selection

This chapter describes aspects of selection that build on the concept of behavioural profiling described in Chapter 2. We give you an opportunity to compare your organization's performance in this area with best practice. Strategically improving the quality of the recruitment and selection process is likely to have a significant impact on the long-term effectiveness of any business. Many difficulties which organizations face with performance management can actually be tracked back to flaws or lack of precision in the process of recruitment and selection.

This chapter commences by looking at the evidence suggesting that the traditional approach to the process of interviewing rarely produces the level of results that might be anticipated. We go on to highlight the application of focused interviewing as a way of enhancing the validity of selection decisions.

Also discussed is the use of assessment centres, focusing in particular on some of the exercises that can be provided in order to test and assess the existence of key competencies and behaviours.

Chapter 4: Coaching

Having explored the performance management perspective in respect of recruitment and selection we move on to consider how it is possible to continue to use the behavioural approach when coaching or developing others to be more effective in their current role.

In this chapter we provide techniques and tools for helping your organization determine the critical skills that individuals need to work on in order to enhance their output effectiveness and, consequently, the organization's performance. We also balance the need to consider behaviours as a focus for coaching with the need to address cognitive processes and motivational issues. How do organizations encourage individuals to change or to confront their lack of confidence or poor attitude? Our experience and research suggests that organizational initiatives often ignore the employee's motivational state. We therefore include our findings in this area.

Additionally, we encourage you to take a broad view of the range of methods that can be used in developing others. All too often, when a performance difficulty emerges the manager reaches for the training course manual and decides which course to send the person on. The return on such an approach is extremely low. Courses are not necessarily the answer and are often selected as a knee-jerk reaction. We highlight the huge variety of developmental methods available and the importance of matching method with the individual's learning style.

Chapter 5: Target setting and performance review

Having looked at coaching as a means of effecting an improvement in performance in the current role, in this chapter we discuss in depth the importance of setting clear performance goals and reviewing performance. We have previously described how organizations traditionally set individual output targets. Here we advocate that a similar level of effort should be placed on the development of input-based targets. In particular we direct attention on the much neglected area of setting targets around behaviours and what have sometimes been described as 'softer' issues. So how, for instance, do we develop a manager's influencing or team working skills? Even where the need is accurately diagnosed, in our experience, managers are often at a loss as to where to start in terms of setting targets for improvement. Although it is by no means easy, it can be done and, in this chapter we build on some of our previously published work in this area (Hale and Whitlam, 1998). Often, managers will raise objections in this area, suggesting that it is not possible to set targets in certain job areas because of supposed uniqueness, but we would challenge such objections. Indeed, if you are seeking to influence key players in the organization to implement such target setting, then this chapter will provide some practical advice.

We also explore the subject of feedback before tracking some of the major developments in the history of performance review or appraisal. This is done on the basis that the skills of target setting and the provision of feedback are often positioned as key skills within the performance appraisal process. In looking at some of the leading-edge developments in this field, we show how Coca-Cola and Xilinx Semiconductor are using a competency approach and 360-degree feedback as a way of improving the quality of review that managers receive. Equally, it can be seen in these case studies how the organization institutionalizes effective performance management.

Chapter 6: Mentoring

This chapter continues the theme of learning and personal development, but now turns to the future, rather than performance improvement in the current role. The principal theme here is that of mentoring. The key considerations in setting up a formalized mentoring programme are discussed, and evidence is provided of how this has been tackled in such organizations as Allied Domecq. A major challenge is to try to re-create, through the formalized mentoring process, the benefits which clearly occur in effective informal mentoring relationships. In line with the recurring theme of competencies discussed throughout the book, this chapter also provides a competency profile of the effective mentor, as well as specific guidance with respect to the perennial problem of matching mentor and mentee.

Chapter 7: Into action

Finally we present a summary of each chapter and raise a number of questions that ask you to compare your organization's or team's approach to performance management. From these comparisons you are encouraged to identify your own output targets for powering up performance management before considering the skills or inputs you need to enhance in order to deliver these targets.

In summary, as a result of reading and working with the model of performance management and integrating those tools and techniques which are relevant to your organization, you are likely to be able to:

- define success in terms of behaviours
- improve recruitment and selection against behaviours
- identify how to improve individual performance in the current role
- develop effective performance appraisal processes and practices
- establish powerful mentoring relationship in order to suppor the longer-term development of individuals.

How to contact the authors

We recognize that, over the years, our thinking – and consequently our books – has been greatly enhanced and enriched by feedback from others. If you would like to discuss any of the issues covered in the book, do contact us in the following way.

Richard Hale
Tel./Fax: +44 (0)117 968 2299
e-mail: rhale@cableinet.co.uk

Peter Whitlam
Tel./Fax: +44(0)1263 515150

References

Argyris, C. and Schön, D.A. (1996), *Organisational Learning II, Theory, Method and Practice*, Reading, MA.: Addison-Wesley.

Hale, R. and Whitlam, P.J. (1998), *Target Setting and Goal Achievement*, London: Kogan Page.

1

THE PROBLEM OF
MEASUREMENT

Human decisions affecting the future . . . cannot depend on strict mathematical expectation.

John Maynard Keynes, Economist 1883–1946

The objectives of Chapter 1 are as follows:

- to provide some historical background on the theme of performance management
- to recognize the importance of measurement in all aspects of both individual and organizational performance
- to explain a key model looking at how individual behavioural inputs contribute to organizational outputs
- to suggest that there is a case for also considering the components of individual behaviour
- to acknowledge the need for a more holistic approach to performance measurement, and therefore management
- to show how an integrated model of performance management provides a basis for understanding the situations in which behavioural technology can be applied
- to consider strategies for influencing others at different levels in your organization in order to support the implementation of effective performance management.

The concept of performance management: history and influences

Performance management is a term which is widely used in organizations, and in particular by human resource professionals; it is a term, however, which will have different definitions and meanings to different people and organizations. A generic definition might be that it is about applying processes, techniques and systems which maintain and improve individuals' performance whilst simultaneously aiming to improve the performance of the organization.

Many organizations claim to operate a performance management system. It is important to emphasize that performance management is not a technique, a procedure or a specific tool, but is more descriptive of a theme, philosophy or approach to managing human resources which manifests itself in a number of behaviours and approaches at all stages of the employee cycle, as described in the subsequent chapters of this book. Simply put, performance management is about trying to improve the performance of individuals and, as a result, that of the whole organization.

In 1992 the Institute of Personnel Management published the results of a major research project into the subject of performance management in the UK (IPM, 1992). Over 1800 employers were surveyed, with a 46 per cent return covering 20 per cent of the UK workforce.

This report found that no consistent definitions of performance management existed amongst organizations professing to operate it, but they did tend to have the following in common:

● They communicated mission statements, business plans and progress towards them.
● They had policies such as Total Quality Management (TQM) and performance-related pay (PRP).
● They focused on senior managers' performance.
● They defined measurable performance targets in terms of outputs, accountabilities and learning.
● They used formal appraisal and linked performance to pay, particularly for senior managers.

The roots of performance management as a concept can be tracked back through a number of organizational development themes from the past. Included here is work study, whereby a job would be broken down into component tasks in a very analytical way. Such analysis provided information to help with supervision, time and cost planning, and data for giving incentives to employees. It can be seen that the competency movement subsequently took an equally analytical approach but has been applied to a broader range of jobs with more applications than work study.

Similarly, merit rating schemes can be related to performance management, in that such schemes have historically attempted to define generic characteristics of effective performance and then provided a rating scale to assess performance against them. However, many such schemes have become discredited because of problems such as:

● the inability to account for the unique aspects of different jobs

- a tendency to use broad headings like 'leadership' and 'teamwork' without clarifying what these terms really mean
- problems with consistency of assessment against broad assessment headings such as 'good', 'below standard' and so on.
- difficulties in measuring more subjective behavioural characteristics and traits.

There were difficulties with management by objectives (MBO) approaches which were popular in the 1960s and 1970s; these are expressed by Dinesh and Palmer (1998). Such approaches attempted to integrate the organizational goals with a hierarchy of objectives cascaded through the organization. Whilst this principle is sound and is, in fact, consistent with some of the characteristics of performance management, difficulties existed related to implementation. Problems were associated with an overemphasis on paperwork and form filling, too many objectives being set, a reliance on hitting numerical targets and a predominantly top-down approach. All too often, the system became more important than the output; the 'tail was wagging the dog'.

As organizations learnt from the problems associated with these ideas, we have seen the emergence of a range of approaches to performance appraisal. Many organizations have realized that operating a system of appraisal effectively means recognizing and dealing with difficulties such as:

- getting the paperwork right
- training managers and appraisers to operate appraisal effectively
- linking appraisal with pay
- dealing with behavioural issues as well as task-related targets.

There was a proliferation of appraisal initiatives throughout the 1980s and 1990s, yet, despite all the variations attempted, no single panacea has yet been found.

Furthermore, the emergence in the late 1980s, and development into the 1990s, of the competency movement has had a significant impact on the evolution of the performance management concept. Basically, the contribution of the competency approach has been to emphasize the importance of being able to define success or 'what a good one looks like' and then being able to measure performance against this. In principle, if one can define a particular job specifically and clearly then this information can be used at various stages in the management of performance, including defining the role, selection, identifying development needs, setting developmental targets, appraising and dealing with poor performance. We consider this to be a fundamental concept, which we expand upon later in the chapter with our own model of performance management.

There have also been national attempts to define the competencies required in different jobs, vocations and professions. Whilst these developments have not been without their difficulties, they have played a significant part in moving our thinking forward and encouraging a more systematic approach to defining success.

It is worth briefly considering some of the organizational development-related initiatives and themes which have emerged in recent years, and how these relate to performance management. The 1980s saw the growth of quality improvement initiatives, many of which stood under the banner of 'Total Quality Management' and which tended to emphasize the following:

● the importance of defining the organization's overall goals and mission
● involvement of all employees in contributing to problem-solving
● a managed approach to performance improvement
● the use of problem-solving groups or quality circles.

The TQM movement has stimulated developments which might include the interest in continuous improvement and business process re-engineering, as organizations have adopted and adapted ideas which might give them a competitive edge. One school of thought has gathered around the concept of the 'learning organization' which suggests that an organization's ability to learn determines its ability to continuously transform, develop and meet the demands of turbulent and competitive markets. Many organizations have realized the value of this message and have introduced policies and practices which encourage learning at all levels, on any subject. One such example is First Direct which encourages and supports learning amongst its employees, regardless of the subject. Why should First Direct support employees who want to learn about yoga or fishing? The bank takes the view that learning to learn is important for all its employees.

The growth of performance management thinking might also be related to a number of social, economic and organizational issues. As we are discussing a broad theme here it is not necessarily possible to pinpoint definitive connections, although it can be helpful in seeking an understanding of performance management to postulate on the main influences.

Increasing competition has driven organizations to look closely at ways of ensuring that individual and team performance is maximized and that it impacts on the performance of the organization as a whole. As organizations have delayered and downsized, the value of the traditional hierarchical organizational structure has been questioned. The public sector has seen a move towards a 'contract culture' – take, for example, the introduction of compulsory competitive tendering and the purchaser–provider split in healthcare in the UK. Equally, many private sector organizations have focused more on the customer and supplier relationship, both internal and external.

An overused buzzword is 'empowerment', some organizations using the word without really being able to define it. Perhaps this is something you recognize in your own organization. However, the empowerment philosophy is about recognizing the benefits which can accrue from truly devolving power to those at the lower levels of the structure who are often closer to the customer or front end of the business. We have also seen a move away from national bargaining and an increasing recognition, in industrial relations, of the need to deal with individuals and to reward them on the basis of their own contribution. As the rate of technological change has increased the number of specialisms in many professions and vocations has risen, with the implication that managers and leaders need to find

effective ways of understanding, measuring, rewarding and enhancing performance.

While the research quoted earlier may not have found a definitive recipe for
success, or even a common definition of performance management, there were a
number of useful conclusions drawn:

- Performance management approaches which allow individuals to identify
  closely with the aims of the organization experience the most success. This
  suggests a need to, first, define the organization's goals and then to communicate them effectively to teams and individuals.
- There is also a need to put more emphasis on recognizing the needs of the
  individual. Many organizations operating performance management systems
  did so because of commercial considerations, which is undoubtedly important, but this was often at the expense of individual considerations.
  Organizations should consider intrinsic needs of employees, such as opportunities for development, as well as extrinsic needs such as remuneration.
- Performance management should be approached in an integrated way, which
  takes account of human resource and wider business activity.
- 'Reward-driven integration' which emphasizes, for instance, performance-
  related pay, is of limited value in isolation. There was no conclusive evidence
  of a causal link between performance-related pay and bottom–line business
  results, but there is a need to address developmental issues before rewarding
  performance. Remuneration forms only part of the equation, and rewards
  should be viewed in a wider sense to include matters such as training and personal development. 'Development-driven integration' which addresses such
  developmental issues is just as important.
- Performance management should be owned by the line manager rather than
  the HR specialist; the HR specialist should provide a corporate approach and
  maintain the system.

'What gets measured gets done'

Undoubtedly, in business, the above statement holds true. For some time organizations have recognized that once a measurement has been defined, then it is possible not only to hold individuals or departments accountable, but it is also equally
useful to deploy such measurements as a basis for control, ongoing planning and,
where applicable, for contingency planning. Traditionally, the measurements
have been centred on what we would refer to as 'hard' issues, such as sales or production. Nowadays, we have increasingly seen organizations attempt to define
other measurements in order to direct attention to key result areas. This has led to
a higher profile for measures such as the customer satisfaction index and the
employee opinion survey.

Most organizations would accept the benefit of measurement – indeed, most, if
not all, commercial organizations would claim it is essential. However, we believe

that, in many organizations, the issue of individual performance measurement has never been successfully resolved. We suggest that individual performance assessment, where it is measured, is often assessed against hard business objectives, and little attention is given to what are often referred to as the 'softer issues'.

In our previous research which was published in *Towards The Virtual Organization* (1997), we identified that successful organizations tended to demonstrate the following common characteristics:

- They demonstrated ongoing concern for their staff.
- They encouraged high levels of participation.
- They placed emphasis on innovation.
- They developed entrepreneurial skills.
- They were highly customer-oriented.
- They encouraged individuals to use influence, rather than authority.
- They ensured all processes were measured.

It is this latter factor which we would like to focus on here. In the highly successful organizations there was seldom a discussion about 'softer' issues and whether or not they should be considered. In these organizations there existed a general assumption that all things were measurable.

It is worth taking a few moments to reflect on this notion of 'soft' issues. The very expression itself seems to suggest something which is ill-defined or nebulous. Equally, it might be construed that 'soft' means less important than 'hard'. We would contend, however, that this is probably more often implied as a way of avoiding having to confront the first difficulty – that of defining the 'soft' issues of performance.

We believe that behaviour is an output. It is visible, it can be seen, it can be observed and, as a consequence, it can be measured. Admittedly, this calls for an analytical approach and a level of skills in understanding behavioural issues, and to many this might seem to involve a great deal of effort and time with very few tangible benefits. However, this need not be the case. We intend to show how, armed with a sound understanding of the principles of behaviour and a number of practical tools and techniques, it is possible to align human resources with organizational needs and then to ensure that people are used to the best of their ability and, furthermore, developed in order to achieve their real potential.

In order to explore this problem of measurement further, a brief case study, illustrating the key problems and difficulties, follows.

CASE STUDY: THE REAL COST OF SUCCESS ?

Across the organization Jim S. was recognized as a successful sales manager and someone who was going places in the organization. Jim regularly achieved most of his sales targets and used to boast to others about the contribution that he made to the profits of the business, claiming to bring $500 000 into the company each year. Jim managed a team of 20 salespeople and it was generally well known that his personal style was autocratic and somewhat confrontational. Certainly, Jim could be charming but he tended to reserve this behaviour for customers. Within the organization Jim had a reputation for being tough and difficult to deal with.

Because of his apparent success, we were asked to spend some time with Jim and put together a personal development plan that would allow him to grow even further in the business.

On our first meeting it became clear that Jim had a personal style that could be described as abrasive. He tended to snap instructions at others and used an unhealthy dose of sarcasm in the way in which he talked. Certainly he was achieving all his sales targets, but it was noticeable that all these targets were hard, quantifiable measurements. For example, Jim was told that he 'must achieve x sales in y period of time'.

On closer examination, it was seen that Jim's team had a high labour turnover. In fact this was running at 25 per cent per year. When challenged on this, he explained that he knew 'he was a hard task master, and if an individual was not up for the job, they would have to walk'.[1]

Part of the assignment involved discussing with Jim what successful performance in his role looked like. However, all he seemed to talk about was sales results. Eventually he agreed, albeit grudgingly, that managerial skills such as developing staff, effective communication and motivation of others were important aspects of his role. There appeared to be an assumption that these things were happening automatically anyway. From discussions with some of his team, it was evident that none of the good practices were taking place. Actually, the way Jim tended to achieve results through his people was by instilling a sense of fear in them. He would coerce them into doing things and force them to cooperate. Evidently the absence of some of the more appropriate behaviours was contributing to the high levels of turnover in his department.

We then turned our attention to his relationships within the organization. Jim seemed to almost pride himself on his ability to alienate others to get what he wanted, and he revelled in the reputation that preceded him in most internal business relationships. He was also oblivious to the fact that, when individuals were alienated, they would seek to 'pay him back' either overtly or covertly.

By now, Jim's real contribution to the business was beginning to look less than exemplary.

Our remedial actions in the above case were, first, to encourage Jim to recognize, and then accept, that achieving sales was an output and, as such, could be achieved by a variety of different routes. In addition, he needed to recognize the inputs or behaviours that made him more likely to achieve results without costing the business money. Having raised his awareness of this, we worked with Jim and, by using a process of 360-degree feedback combined with individual coaching

1   It should be noted that it has been estimated that if an employee leaves an organization within the first year, it has probably cost the organization three times the employee's annual salary. This figure might appear excessive, but it is taken to include the costs of advertising, recruitment and training. Additionally, research reports in the UK have estimated that not getting things right first time in a manufacturing organization may cost that organization as much as 10 per cent of its turnover, whereas in a service organization this might rise to 20 per cent.

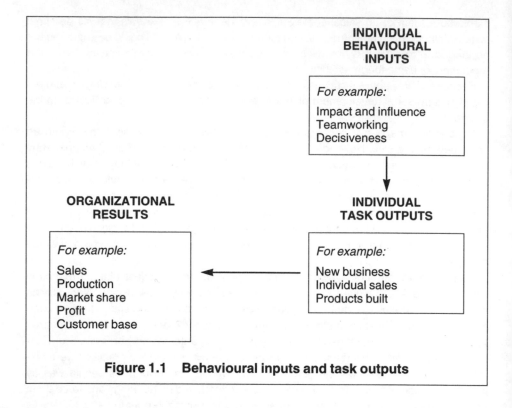

Figure 1.1   Behavioural inputs and task outputs

and counselling, we were able to achieve significant positive change. What is more, the 360-degree feedback was based very specifically around the behavioural requirements that had been identified as critical for Jim's job, and the coaching programme was also centred around developing skills in key behaviours.

So we are arguing then that there is a significant difference between behavioural inputs and task outputs. This can be demonstrated most clearly by the model in Figure 1.1. In this model we show that organizational results are simply the output of a number of individual task outputs. What we mean by this is that the organization's performance can be seen as the result of the combined output of all of its people. We would accept, of course, that other factors, such as its political, economic and technological context, do influence the organization's performance, but here we are most concerned with those aspects of performance which are more controllable at the individual and organizational level. The key part of the model, though, is that the outputs achieved by an individual are the result of a number of behaviours. So, for instance, impact and persuasion might be key behaviours which lead to a salesperson making sales (outputs). Or decisiveness could help a production manager decide which machinery to invest in, which might result (when combined with other behaviours) in increased production output.

This suggests that the challenge is to identify the behaviours that are critical to success in a job role, which has been the thinking underpinning the competency movement which saw rapid growth during the 1990s. Many have recognized the importance of correctly identifying the key behaviours required in a job role. This has also led to attempts in many professions and work domains to identify generic competencies which can be applied in different organizations. For example, the Management Charter Initiative in the UK attempted to devise a competency framework for the role of management. This met with mixed results, many organizations eventually realizing that there is no substitute for actually looking at one's own organization rather than at an imported 'list' of behaviours.

Over recent years we have worked with many organizations and have espoused the competency approach, contributing to this movement on a national and international level. We have seen client organizations such as Coca-Cola, Allied Domecq and Motorola embrace this thinking and reap the benefits of applying this approach in a number of areas of human resource management, and, later in the book, we share some of the key lessons learnt from this experience.

It is worth adding, however, that our own thinking in this area has developed since we first ventured into the world of competencies. We would now build on the model presented in Figure 1.1. We believe – and this is supported by much experimental research in the areas of cognitive and social psychology – that individual behaviour is actually the output of a number of other preceding factors, namely:

- thinking
- feelings
- attitudes/beliefs
- social awareness.

Consider the case of a manager who is failing to perform effectively in terms of output. Say he is the marketing manager responsible for the development of a marketing strategy for a new brand. We might look beyond his task output to concentrate on his actual behaviour in order to identify where he is failing to deliver with respect to developing new marketing strategies. The behavioural input that we note is lacking is to do with creativity and strategic thinking. Moving back through the model to look at the factors that contribute to individual behaviour might be particularly revealing. What we might find is that, in terms of logical *thinking*, the manager has an understanding of the required approach to the new marketing strategy but has evaluated it as being technically flawed. If we were to consider his *feelings* we might discover that he actually feels angry about the fact that he has not been properly consulted regarding the changes which are taking place. Furthermore, if we were able to identify his *attitudes and beliefs*, we might find that there is a clash between his own ethical beliefs and how he sees the organization operating – in other words, he considers some of the new ways of working to be inherently unethical.

As far as *social awareness* is concerned, social psychologists would argue that much of our behaviour is influenced by the fact that we operate in a social environment with other people observing our behaviour. This will affect the way in which we behave; we will modify or adjust our behaviour depending on who will see it and what we think of them. This means that the marketing manager above

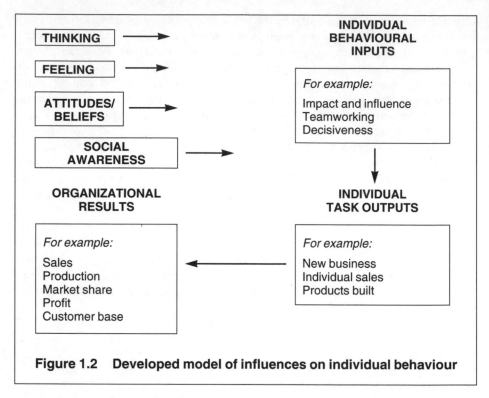

Figure 1.2   Developed model of influences on individual behaviour

might not overtly demonstrate disagreement with the new marketing strategies because he may not wish to be seen as a controversial figure. Or he might be inhibited by the fact that his boss is very harsh on dissenters and wields a great deal of power. Whilst he does not display open dissent, he may choose to downplay this aspect of his job and concentrate on other issues.

As we can see, then the whole issue of performance measurement and management is fraught with difficulties and is more complex than it might first appear. Increasingly, performance has to be managed in a changing organizational environment, and this leads us to believe that there is a particularly strong case for addressing individual behaviours and, beyond this, attitudes, feelings, beliefs and the social context in which people are expected to perform.

We have seen many organizations try to bring about organizational culture change and maximize performance by taking an entirely organizational view. So the new business strategy is decided, the structure is changed and a new set of organizational values are announced. Unsurprisingly, this alone will have little bearing on individual behaviour.

So we would propose a significant addition to the model presented earlier in Figure 1.1. Figure 1.2 shows the more complete picture, recognizing the precedent components to individual behaviour.

A working model of performance management

We have explored the distinction between behavioural inputs and task outputs and, overall, we propose that there is a need to take a balanced look at both when considering the measurement or definition of performance.

Our working model of performance management suggests that if we are able to measure behaviour with some degree of scientific reliability, then we can reap the benefits at all stages of the employment process. Figure 1.3 shows a model which presents the employment process as a cycle.

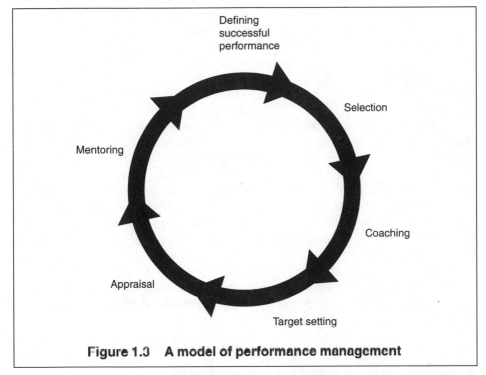

Figure 1.3   A model of performance management

In order to effectively manage performance we advocate that the organization initially explores and identifies the behaviours critical to the role. This goes some way to ensuring the right fit between the individual and the role. You will have undoubtedly seen the situation where an individual takes on a new job role which, on the face of it, appears ideal, only to find that within a few weeks they, or the organization, realize that it was a terrible mistake. In our experience, this scenario is all too common, and it is usually due to the fact that only the more obvious criteria such as salary, level and title have been taken into consideration. The really important issues such as what behaviours, skills, attitudes or values are required are ignored.

At the selection stage we advocate a rigorous process using a defined behavioural profile and focused behavioural interviewing in order to measure an individual's capability for the role.

Next, in the model, we suggest that individuals will want help in determining their development needs, and the important consideration here is how coaching can be used to support development in the current job role. In many cases, the 'flooding' approach is used where employees are simply thrown in at the deep end and expected to sink or swim. Such individuals are given no help in determining their real development needs and little meaningful help in meeting them.

The next stage is the need to set meaningful targets and goals which the individual can work towards. These can be formulated around the input behaviours which are identified as critical for success in the role or the output measures. Both involve giving people the opportunity to perform whilst letting them know how they are doing. This helps in keeping individuals motivated through the provision of relevant feedback, work and development opportunities.

Performance review in the context of performance management entails more than just the regular (normally annual or six-monthly) formal performance appraisal. It should, we suggest, be a continual process of providing focused feedback regarding performance, including strengths and areas for further development.

Next, in the model, we distinguish between coaching, which concerns helping the individual to improve in the current role, and the need to focus on the future. Focusing on the future involves helping the individual identify those skills that will need to be developed in order to support development beyond the current role. This calls for mentoring skills, and there is a considerable body of evidence to suggest that effective mentoring relationships often come about informally. However, we have researched the subject of mentoring and found that it is possible to apply many of the principles seen in informal mentoring to a formal mentoring programme.

In the following chapters we will unpack this model in more detail and show how organizations can take a proactive role in managing performance, allowing you to identify how you can power up your organizations' approach to performance management.

Exerting influence within your organization

For many who are responsible for establishing a culture of performance management in their organization there may be no problem in terms of individual commitment to the concept and approach. However, often the challenge is concerned with how to influence and persuade others to change their approach to performance management. It is reasonable to expect that others will have their own priorities and motives, or even values, which will impact on their disposition towards the performance management philosophy described here. In this section we use just three different types of individual to consider the barriers you are likely to encounter and look at how you might identify their perspective more clearly and influence them in order to create momentum within the organization. In the final chapter of the book we ask you to consider specifically who you have to influence and provide you with the opportunity to use the approach described below to develop your plan of action.

If you are working in a human resource management role, then it is important at one level to work closely with the line in order to support the development of a performance management culture. This will mean identifying where there is evidence of good practice, building on this and spreading such practice to other parts of the organization. In any change initiative you might encounter three categories of response as shown in Figure 1.4. Here we show that there will always be a minority of what are described as 'terrorists', or those who will seek to sabotage or destroy any attempt to implement change in the organization. These people will either overtly challenge and resist any change efforts or they will appear willing while moaning and infecting others with their negative attitude behind the scenes. Ironically some of these people will have been with the organization for some time. In the middle is the critical mass or that majority of people who are actually not too worried about the change initiative one way or the other. These people are reasonably open-minded and willing to listen, and the aim in any organizational change initiative is to get the critical mass moving in the direction of the goal or vision – in this case, moving towards effective performance management strategies and practices. On the right-hand side of the figure we show what we describe as the 'early adopters'. These people will adopt any new initiative with enthusiasm and a sense of ownership.

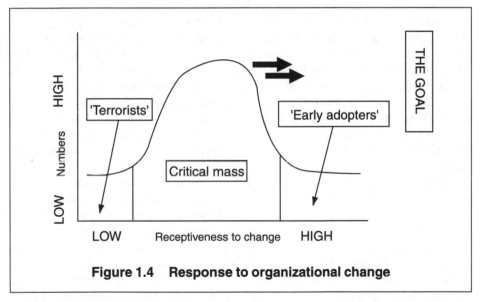

Figure 1.4   Response to organizational change

Traditionally, the supposedly effective approach to organizational change has been to direct effort towards winning over the terrorists on the grounds that by turning these people around it would be easier to bring about change. Unfortunately there are many cases where such efforts to bring about change have resulted in failure simply because dealing with the terrorists takes up an undue amount of time and effort. We believe, from our own work in implementing performance management in organizations, that time is actually better spent working with the early adopters on the basis that once they have been won over they will then go and spread their good news regarding the new approach to others in the organization. Marketeers use a similar strategy whereby they will target those they describe as 'key opinion informers' who buy a product early in its life cycle and then encourage the wider population to experience the benefits.

We used this approach in one organization by running a pilot appreciation programme with hand-picked early adopters at the beginning of a major performance management initiative. The programme gave those managers attending an appreciation of the performance management model as described here and allowed them to consider how the approach suggested could be built into the organization's systems and practices. In this way they left the programme with enthusiasm and were able to generate demand for the programme from others. A further clever approach to encouraging buy-in in other ways was taken by the global human resource directorate. For instance, one area of weakness that had been identified through the global employee opinion survey was that of performance improvement coaching and ongoing employee development. The introduction of the performance management programme was positioned as building on the current system and was sold as a response to the needs identified by employees through the opinion survey. In this way they overcame the common difficulty of their efforts being interpreted as 'just another initiative'; it was positioned as a response to the opinion of the majority.

So, on a strategic level, you might think about how to move the critical mass of the organization towards improving its approach to performance management. However, at a more tactical level it is important to think through the perspectives of those you are trying to influence, and the approach we recommend here is the use of the perspective specification. Here we see things through the other person's eyes or, to quote the old native American expression, to 'walk in the other man's shoes'. This can either be done informally or more formally by drawing up a perspective specification as shown in Figure 1.5. As can be seen, this helps us identify the barriers and should lead to the preparation of responses to overcome them.

Three examples are shown in Figure 5.1 – the perspective specification, for a senior director, a line manager and a team member. Clearly, these are simply short examples. In reality we would suggest you draw up your own unique perspective specification relevant to those you have to influence in your organization.

These sample perspective specifications demonstrate the importance of at least trying to see the implementation of performance management from the other person's perspective. The objections you are likely to meet in this sort of situation are many but, thankfully, tend to be fairly predictable. So you might like to think about how to overcome such objections as:

- 'It will cost too much.'
- 'The timing is not right.'
- 'We have tried it before.'
- 'Mr/s X will not like the idea.'

Perspective Specification: Senior Director	
Perspective	
We cannot be seen to be spending a lot of money on another human resources-led initiative. Possibly driven by need for achievement, recognition and results.	
Possible objections/questions	**Possible responses**
How will this affect the bottom line (profit etc)?	Will help employee turnover. Should be seen as a long-term investment. Consider cost of low morale.
Will it be seen as another HR initiative?	Need to co-opt your support in launching it? Could you provide a strategic input at workshops or in writing?

Perspective Specification: Line Manager	
Perspective	
May feel caught between senior management and own team. Motivated by own functional/professional factors. Could see performance management as just another fad.	
Possible objections/questions	**Possible responses**
This is more of an HR/personnel issue.	Challenge this – clarify role of HR/personnel in facilitating and supporting.
Generally my people are performing OK.	Is there no scope for them to do even better?

Perspective Specification: Team Member	
Perspective	
May feel limited in ability to influence events. May be concerned about equity and fair treatment and recognition for his/her contribution.	
Possible objections/questions	**Possible responses**
Will I get an increase in my pay?	Pay is only part of the performance management strategy. It is about getting people to perform to the best of their ability, and to achieve their potential and contribute to the organization.
I could do with going on some courses.	Courses may be appropriate but there are lots of other ways of developing – for instance, through coaching and mentoring.

Figure 1.5   Perspective specifications

- 'I need time to think about it.'
- 'Good in theory but not in practice.'
- 'I need to consult . . .'

Summary

This chapter has covered the need to clearly define successful performance in terms of behavioural inputs as well as performance outputs. We have argued that, by taking a more structured approach to the measurement of performance, we are then in a better position to manage it at all stages of the performance management cycle. Implementing a performance management strategy is far from simple, however, and in the final section we considered some of the hurdles which need to be overcome as far as influencing others is concerned. Next we will move on to look at the use of behavioural technology in the recruitment and selection process. Before we do, however, you might like to pause for thought . . . .

PAUSE FOR THOUGHT

- *How is performance measured in your organization?*
- *Is there a balanced approach to defining behavioural inputs and task outputs?*
- *How well are roles or jobs defined?*
- *Are targets set against behaviours inputs as well as outputs?*
- *How effective are systems and processes for reviewing performance?*
- *In what ways are people helped to improve and develop?*
- *How do you feel that different parties will react to the changes you would intend to implement in the area of performance management?*
- *What values do they hold? How can you appeal to those values?*
- *Who are the early adopters? How could you co-opt their support?*

References

Dinesh, D. and Palmer, E. (1998), 'MBO and balance scorecard. Will Rome fall again?', *Management Decision*, **36**(6), pp. 363–9.

Hale, R. and Whitlam, P.J. (1995), *The Power of Personal Influence*, Maidenhead: McGraw-Hill.

Hale, R. and Whitlam, P.J. (1997), *Towards the Virtual Organization*, Maidenhead: McGraw-Hill.

IPM (1992), *Performance Management in the UK – An Analysis of the Issues*, London: IPM.

2

DEFINING SUCCESSFUL PERFORMANCE

Achieving good performance is a journey not a destination.

Kenneth Blanchard (1984)

The objectives of this chapter are as follows:

- to critically evaluate some of the traditional tools used for defining jobs and roles
- to identify a range of techniques that can be used to define successful performance
- to discuss the concept and importance of triangulation in research
- to describe in detail the use of structured interviews incorporating:
  - diary technique
  - critical incident analysis
  - repertory grid analysis
- to consider the use of observation in defining success, and to discuss the use of other sources of data
- to explain the mechanism for developing a Skills Analysis Questionnaire.

Here we continue to explore the importance of measurement as a prerequisite for effective performance management and give you some ideas for defining the skills really required for a role. Although this is the first step in the effective manage-ment of performance, it is not the end of the journey. In Chapter 1 we suggested that, unless you can first define successful performance and then measure aspects of that performance, the process of performance management becomes meaning-less. Determining what success looks like and what skills are required represents the first stage in the model of managing performance as already presented in Figure 1.3.

In this chapter we concentrate on the practical skills and techniques that support the production of a behavioural profile – in other words, what successful performance 'looks like'. Once the real skills of the role have been identified and described, you should then be able to determine individual areas of development need.

A behavioural profile comprises a statement of the key skills, behaviours or competencies – that is, the inputs – which a person requires to be successful in a role. We suggest a variety of thorough, yet practical, enquiry methods that fall within the qualitative research school. Essentially we advocate the application of a scientific, yet pragmatic, approach. In defining successful performance – either of a role you are seeking to fill, or an existing role – there are a number of different techniques that can be used. These are described later. However, first, we need to say a few words about triangulation.

The concept of triangulation

Triangulation describes the process of seeking data or information from at least three independent sources. In fact the greater the number of different sources the greater the confidence we can have in the findings.

Traditionally, in considering the definition of jobs, data has been collected using just one method of collection and analysis. This was probably sufficient when job roles were clear-cut and all that was required was to define key roles, responsibilities and tasks. However, as job roles have become increasingly dynamic, subject to change and ambiguous, a need has developed to consider the definition from a number of vantage points and perspectives. To meet this need we describe here a range of tools and techniques for defining successful performance. The literature on research methods would suggest there a number of different types of triangulation, namely:

- **Data triangulation** – where we collect the accounts from different individuals who will have an opinion or perspective. So, with the techniques described below, we would use them with the current job-holder, the subordinates in defining their manager's job, the manager's boss and perhaps peers as well. This might sound like overkill but, remember, the more perspectives – that is, the more you can triangulate – the more reliable the ultimate job profile.
- **Method triangulation** – where different methods are used to collect information. Using a variety of methods to collect data minimizes the disadvantages and weaknesses arising when a single method is used on its own. So below we describe methods ranging from critical incident analysis to the 'day-in-the-life technique' and suggest that the more methods used the more reliable will be your subsequent findings.
- **Investigator triangulation** – where a number of investigators from different backgrounds are used in gathering the data. This helps overcome the problem of bias whereby the investigator will either consciously or subconsciously interpret incoming data from their own, rather than an objective,

perspective. Whilst we recognize that this might be problematic, both organizationally and politically, in organizations seeking to define roles, it may nevertheless be possible.

Methods and techniques for defining the job role

Probing the role profile or job description

Many organizations put time and effort into defining the key accountabilities or key result areas within a job description. Often these accountabilities relate to successful achievement of broader business plans. For instance, a key accountability statement might say that a manager is 'To build up-to-date, accurate databases and to use this information as a basis for seeking and acquiring new customers'.

If we were to take this statement, which is essentially about outputs, we were to simply ask the question 'How?' we would start to gain a picture of how success is achieved. Eventually we would begin to arrive at the behavioural inputs required. The above statement can be seen to suggest that the job incumbent would probably require the following behavioural skill-set:

- planning and organization
- attention to detail
- data management
- initiative
- persuasion.

Further examination might suggest that there is a requirement for such skills as judgement and even decisiveness. Indeed, in the above example we have only used one statement of an accountability or key result area. In practice we would use a similar process against all the given key result areas in order to establish what behavioural skills are required in order to achieve success. This leads to the production of a behavioural profile. In the context of selection, such a profile moves the concept of the person specification forward, beyond the usual measures of qualifications, years of experience and achievements and into the realms of the key skills and behaviours required in the role.

Probing a job description is a useful and simple technique. But, used alone, it may not be sufficient to build a robust behavioural profile.

Interviewing

The structured interview probably provides the most valuable approach to defining successful performance. Such an approach can be used with a post-holder or those who work closely, or deal, with the incumbent – for example, peers, managers and team members.

The design of a structured interview should contain the following sorts of question that will provide valuable indicators as to the key behaviours:

- 'Describe the overall purpose of the role.'
- 'What are the key tasks and activities?'
- 'How much time is spent on these tasks?'
- 'What are the most common problems in the role?'
- 'How are these problems managed?'
- 'What is the most difficult part of the job?'
- 'How do you cope with this?'
- 'How has the role changed in the past year?'
- 'How will it be different in three years' time?'

Examination of the responses from a range of interested parties and comparison with data drawn from the probing process described above will lead to a better understanding.

Within such a structured interview it is possible to incorporate a number of additional techniques. These may include the following:

- critical incident analysis
- diary or day-in-the-life technique
- repertory grid.

These techniques can be designed into the structured interview, and so strengthen findings through the triangulation of results.

Critical incident analysis

With this technique the interviewer asks the interviewee or job-holder to focus on a specific incident and to explain it in depth. Our own preferred mechanism for doing this is to ask the job incumbent the following sort of question:

'What has been the most difficult challenge you have faced in the last three months?'

This question can then be followed up with a number of supplementary probing questions – for example:

- 'What caused this to happen?'
- 'What happened next?'
- 'Who else was involved?'
- 'What did you do?'

The important thing to remember, when using this technique, is that it is designed to help us understand the key behaviours necessary for success in the role. So, when it is used in the context described here, it is about *defining* performance, which is not to be confused with assessing performance. In other words, the focus is more on the requirements in the role rather than on individual performance.

With critical incident questioning the key rule is probe, probe, and probe some more. In our experience with critical incident analysis, it will probably take between 15–30 minutes to fully explore one incident.

EXAMPLE OF CRITICAL INCIDENT ANALYSIS

Interviewer: Can you think of a big challenge or major problem you faced recently? Take your time ... if one does not spring to mind then we can come back to it later.

Interviewee: Well actually there was the problem we had last week when the computer system crashed. I'm not sure whether that is really relevant.

Interviewer: It may well be. It depends really on what your role was in dealing with the problem. Tell me more.

Interviewee: Well, the hard drives went down on the network and we were simply without access to our systems for over a day.

Interviewer: How did you cope?

Interviewee: I obviously had no choice in the matter but to accept there were some technical issues that only the technical support department could deal with. However, that was no excuse for sitting around twiddling our thumbs. Besides I had a department to run and people who needed deploying productively. Every hour they are unassigned to a project they are costing us money.

Interviewer: So what specifically did you do?

Interviewee: I got on to technical support as soon as I realized we could not fix the problem ourselves.

Interviewer: So you tried to sort it out yourself first then?

Interviewee: Yes, I suppose so. In actual fact, I put our latest graduate recruit on to it. He has just joined and is quite strong technically. I am trying to involve him more now that he has been here a few months. Anyway he had no joy so I realized there comes a point where you have to look outside. The technical support staff came down and said they would have to put the system out of operation for at least a day.

Interviewer: That must have been pretty frustrating.

Interviewee: It certainly was. But it is no good losing your cool over these things, so I went into action mode. I put the customer service people on to visits with some of the sales team. In the end that worked out quite well because they ended up meeting some of the new contacts who they only normally deal with over the telephone.

Clearly, the conversation shown above would have continued for some time, but you can see from the extract shown that the interviewer's role is to keep the job-holder focused on what they actually did in practice. The more they say in relation to the question, the more they reveal about their own behaviour and the activities or behaviour which were critical in the job. You may have worked out that, from the discussion above, some of the key skills would have been:

- controlled demeanour – staying calm under pressure
- coordination of people – ensuring members of the team are deployed effectively
- flexibility – coping with changing circumstances
- initiative – trying to deal with a problem before seeking external help.

If the critical incident is well chosen it will reveal a wealth of information regarding the behaviour required and displayed by the job-holder.

After the interview, the data is sifted and the key behaviour identified. At this stage it will be possible to pinpoint which behaviours have to be displayed by the manager the most. If these behaviours are then identified as important as a result of using other techniques, in accordance with the concept of triangulation, we will know that we have some reliable data to incorporate into the behavioural profile.

The following extracts from Evert Gummeson's *Qualitative Methods in Management Research* (1991) support our view of the real value of this technique:

> The Critical Incident Technique (CIT) is a method for coming close to direct observation but avoiding some of its hardships. (p.117)

> It is an inductive method where no hypotheses are needed and the incidents, as they appear in the answers, are allowed to form patterns that the researcher can develop into concepts and theories. (p.118)

Gummeson goes on to describe how, in one reported use of the technique to investigate the role of the customer service person across three industries – hotels, restaurants and airlines – 131 employees were interviewed producing 355 usable incidents. Respondents were asked to remember real customer interactions and provide enough detail for the interviewer to visualize each situation. Clearly, for many job roles, and for managerial work in particular, it is often impractical to observe all situations directly and the critical incident technique can provide a worthy substitute for direct observation.

Diary or day-in-the-life technique

This technique can yield a great deal of data if carried out correctly. In some ways it is similar to the critical incident analysis, in that it works from accounts of behaviour as described by the subject.

With this technique we usually start by clearly explaining to the job incumbents that we are going to try to understand exactly what they do in their role, and that we are going to use this information to produce a behavioural profile. We further explain that we will ask them to describe a typical day for us. We acknowledge that there probably is no such thing as 'typical', but ask them to provide us with a composite day. If the individual has difficulty with this, then we ask them to describe what they did yesterday or the day before.

In using this technique, it is important that the individual starts at the beginning of the day and goes right through to the end. In addition, we usually ask them to specify how long they spend on each activity.

It is best not to interrupt the people while they are describing their day. Once they have finished you must review what they have said and probe for more detail. Once again, it is important to keep asking questions which reveal more information about the skills or behaviours involved, such as:

- 'What did you do?'
- 'How did you do it?'
- 'What was easy/difficult?'
- 'Who else was involved?'
- 'What was their role compared to yours?'

With this technique make allowances for the fact that if the individual is describing what they think they do rather than what they have actually done, using an actual day may result in the possibility of them unwittingly presenting a distorted impression, highlighting certain activities and downplaying others. None the less, this approach has high face validity with the person being interviewed and can certainly provide a rich source of data for triangulation purposes.

EXAMPLE OF DIARY TECHNIQUE

Interviewer:	Could you describe specifically what you did yesterday?
Interviewee:	Well it was another one of those crazy days where I didn't seem to stop from the moment I came in until going home.
Interviewer:	So what literally happened from the start?
Interviewee:	Well I came in early – I'm usually first in as I like to check the lay of the land before everyone else arrives and I always start with picking up my e-mail and checking the post.
Interviewer:	So what did that lead to yesterday?
Interviewee:	As always, there is a lot of junk mail and less relevant stuff. I manage to identify that pretty quickly – sometimes I just delete before opening the e-mail. Then there will be some really critical information. Yesterday it was an announcement from corporate headquarters regarding our quarterly figures and a new contract for a major design project.
Interviewer:	So what did you do with that information?
Interviewee:	I immediately copied it to the team and planned a meeting of those who were in to discuss the implications for us. I have learned from experience that people can easily feel ignored if they hear about this sort of thing through the grapevine.
Interviewer:	So did the meeting take place right away?
Interviewee:	No, it happened mid-morning. Actually, I needed to check on some of the figures with my boss before the meeting because there was a bit of ambiguity.
Interviewer:	So you went to see your boss?

Interviewee:	No I called him up. He was away on business and I wouldn't normally bother him, but this was important.

In this example we can see that the discussion has only got as far as mid-morning yet we can already pick out a number of key behaviours and skills which the job-holder has to display such as:

- planning
- prioritization
- business awareness
- initiative
- persuasion.

We now move on to the use of repertory grids and their role in defining good performance.

Repertory grid

As a technique the use of repertory grid again has its roots in qualitative research. Here we present a pragmatic approach utilizing the benefits of the more detailed technique. The repertory grid technique was originally developed in the field of social research and is still widely used, although in its purest form it is somewhat complex and difficult to use.

With this technique we can research a particular job without having to interview the actual incumbent. It is possible, for instance, to interview a person reporting to the job-holder, a peer or the person's manager. We could, of course, interview an actual job-holder regarding their role too.

Repertory grid is basically a method of paired comparisons. A limiting factor is the theoretical need to have at least seven people carrying out the same role. We have overcome this problem by using a more pragmatic approach using just three or five comparable roles. However, when we do this, we triangulate our findings with the results of other enquiry methods.

You first need to identify an individual who knows at least three or five individuals who are doing, or have done, the job you are investigating. The odd number is important. It should be noted that it is not necessary for the person carrying out interview research to know the full name or identity of these individuals. Indeed, in many cases, the person being interviewed may want to ensure anonymity.

You then take, say, five pieces of paper, one for each individual known to the interviewee, and ask them to write one name on to each piece of paper. Next, lay the pieces of paper out in front of the interviewee asking them to consider all of the individuals in turn and to hand over the piece of paper which has the name of the person who they believe is the best performer in the role. Mark this as B1 and remove it from the other pieces of paper. Repeat this process but, this time, ask the interviewee to select the person who they feel is the worst performer. Take this paper and mark it W2. Repeat the process again, marking the best of the remaining performers B2 and the worst of the remaining performers W1. At this point there will be one name remaining which should be marked as A or average.

You will have now ranked performance of the five individuals in the role you are investigating. We have allocated names to help you understand the principle:

B1   John
B2   Sally
A   Ken
W1   Jenny
W2   Bill

You are now ready to begin the analysis. Explain to the interviewee that you are going to put in front of them two pieces of paper and that you will ask them to talk about the two individuals. In effect you are going to ask them to compare and contrast aspects of their performance. This is done for all the individuals using a comparison sequence as follows:

B1 v. W2
B2 v. W1
B1 v. A
A v. W2

From the perspective of the interviewees, they are describing real people and providing real examples of behaviour. In our experience, some people find it immensely difficult to compare and contrast different individuals. We have worked around this by providing a few prompting questions which can help – although, in a pure sense, we acknowledge that such questions could be leading.

- 'What is the principal difference between these two individuals?'
- 'What are their individual strengths?'
- 'What are their individual weaknesses?'
- 'What is the difference between these two in the way they manage others?'
- 'What are the differences in their financial or numerical skills?'
- 'What are the differences in their technical skills?'
- 'How do they do manage their time?'
- 'How would they both manage in a crisis?'
- 'If they were both given an important project what is the difference in how they would go about it?'

It is important to remember that these questions should only be used if the interviewee seems unable to provide critical analysis. While the interviewee is responding, either with or without prompting, the answers should be recorded in full. We have found that the easiest way to do this is by simply recording positive and negative characteristics separately. An example of this is shown below.

Positive	Negative
First in, last out	Complains about things
Knows what she wants to achieve	Poor at putting ideas across
Can talk to anybody	Can not decide quickly enough
Works well under pressure	Untidy office
Has regular reviews	Misses things
Always tells it straight	Steals the glory from others

In the above example it can be seen that both the positive and negative character-istics provide us with valuable data. The positives clearly suggest the types of behaviour that we are looking for, whereas the negatives provide contra-indicators or characteristics to be avoided. Obviously, you are recording positive and neg-ative indicators from your own perspective – for example, some one else might see 'first in last out' as a negative revealing an inability to manage time. Detailed analysis of these responses would suggest the types of behaviour that contribute to successful performance in the role. From the list above these might include the following:

● energy
● positive attitudes
● goal orientation
● persuasiveness/good verbal skills
● decisiveness
● tolerance of stress
● self-organization
● management control
● attention to detail
● integrity.

The above brief example shows only a fraction of the volume of data that can be obtained by using this technique. In reality, after a few questions responses tend to become repetitious. In the subsequent analysis these repetitive responses should be recorded and, eventually, it will be those responses that are most frequently recorded, providing a basis for building the final behavioural profile for the role.

In a recent series of repertory grid interviews conducted for a leading-edge high-technology organization, Xilinx, a total of 80 different behaviours were identified. Clearly, it would be unmanageable to work with so many behaviours, but it was possible to use all these behaviours in the construction of a Skills Analysis Questionnaire. This is discussed later.

Observation

Evidently the use of observation provides many opportunities for the accurate identification of critical behaviours; however, as a general rule, observation is best undertaken by someone who is experienced in using such an approach to identify behaviours. In part, this is because less experienced individuals may not necessarily have the relevant conceptual understanding of behavioural technology to enable them to quickly identify and categorize the behaviours that are being manifested.

Another downside to the use of observation is that it tends to be highly time-consuming. Typically, we have found that it takes around six to eight hours with the individual to collect sufficient data. In addition, there is the potential difficulty that your very presence as an observer will influence the activity or behaviour of the person being observed. They could, for instance, behave differently from usual in order to impress you.

Our approach to observation, therefore, is to spend a typical day with the job incumbent and to try to blend into the background and be as unobtrusive as possible. The observation process does not take place continually; rather, it tends to be undertaken in short bursts of a maximum of 40 minutes. Beyond that time, we find that our ability to concentrate diminishes rapidly.

With observation, you should try to record the specific behaviours that are witnessed. Where the same behaviours are identified in different situations, this should be recorded, allowing subsequent accurate content analysis of the data.

Social psychologists would suggest that most of us tend to adjust our behaviour depending on whom we are with and on the impression we wish to convey. Clearly, there is a danger with observation that this might be the case. This means that a manager might work particularly hard at demonstrating behaviour viewed as good practice – say, planning, organizing and effective time management – although this is generally a less important aspect of carrying out their job. However, the same might be said of self-reporting techniques, such as the critical incident analysis and diary technique previously described, in which people have a tendency to over-report positive characteristics and underreport negative characteristics.

Observation does, however, provide real evidence of behaviour whether or not it has been adapted because of a particular situation, and, in this sense, its value should not be underestimated. Again, the principle of triangulation should be adopted and evidence from observation compared with that from other sources and techniques.

There are often opportunities to unobtrusively observe behaviour when conducting research with an individual, as can be seen in the case study below.

CASE STUDY: UNOBTRUSIVE OBSERVATION IN THE COURSE OF RESEARCH

We were conducting research into the changing role of the branch manager in a national bank in the UK. The aim of the project was to identify the key competencies that were relevant for the future. It was recognized that there would be a requirement for a different breed of manager as the business was becoming more focused, the financial services market was being liberated, technology was advancing and customers were becoming more demanding. Indeed, the balance of power in the customer relationship was changing as customers recognized that they had more choice regarding which bank they chose to patronize.

The research project entailed the following stages:

- Identify key behaviours required in the future by conducting research interviews with a cross-section of managers, including representatives considered to be high, average and low performers.
- Draw up a behavioural profile for the role of branch manager.
- Develop a Skills Analysis Questionnaire that could be used to assess managers against the new behavioural profile.[1]
- Validate the profile and the Skills Analysis Questionnaire by testing it with other managers and comparing results with other assessment instruments such as performance appraisal.

In the course of the interviews with branch managers in their different locations, it was possible to observe a number of behaviours. Given below are two examples of observations made of, first, a low-performing manager and, second, a high performer.

The low-performing manager invited the researcher into his office which was positioned at the back of the branch out of sight from the front desk and customers. Despite the fact that the office was quite small, the manager had positioned his office furniture in a classic power set-up with a top desk set in a T-shape above a lower-level table. The researcher was kept waiting for 15 minutes beyond the scheduled start of the meeting before the manager's secretary escorted him in. The manager made no attempt at small talk and conducted the meeting in a contractual and minimalist manner, simply answering questions that were asked and showing little understanding or interest in the project as a whole. It was observed that the manager had a very condescending style in dealing with his staff and was also overtly critical of his head office. When the researcher asked about methods used for identifying business opportunities, a very primitive manual card index system was demonstrated. Furthermore, when this manager was asked about how he saw the business developing in the future, he became very uneasy as evidenced by his physical behaviour and difficulty in giving a response. This style contrasted dramatically with the observations that were made of the high-performing manager.

The high-performing manager had positioned his office close to the front desk and counter. He was fully prepared for the meeting and spent some time at the start of the meeting, which began punctually, creating rapport and showing a genuine interest in the project. He was at ease when discussing the future of the business and demonstrated his use of technology in managing customer information. Part way through the meeting he asked the researcher to move to one side so that he could see over his shoulder. When asked why, he revealed that he had positioned his chair so that he could see out of the office to the customer service counters and constantly scanned to find out which customers were coming into the branch so that he could spot the most important customers and make sure that he came out of his office to meet personally with them.

---

1   Subsequently the profile was used for the purposes of recruitment and assessment of candidates for future roles. This aspect of the project is covered in more detail in Chapter 3.

Observation alone in the above examples provided some powerful supporting evidence of behaviours which could be used to support findings from the formal research. In summary, observation helped identify the following positive requirements and contra-indicators.

- **Positive behaviours:**
  - preparation
  - rapport–building
  - customer orientation
  - vision
- **Contra–indicators:**
  - status–consciousness
  - resistance to change
  - tactical thinking
  - contractual approach

Skills Analysis Questionnaires

The use of questionnaire methodology to help define roles can be a useful means of ensuring an objective approach. This approach can provide the researcher with invaluable information which can then inform the entire performance management process.

Our specific approach is to design and develop an instrument that we call the Skills Analysis Questionnaire. This sort of questionnaire might be broken down into sections – for instance:

- **Individual skills.** This section would comprise questions concerning behaviours that are probably more personality–related and could include, for instance, competencies such as decisiveness, integrity and stamina. These behaviours are particularly important because they are the least easy to train. If the research indicates that some of these behaviours are critical, then this clearly has serious implications for resourcing; there is a need to recruit people who have these skills. If this proves difficult then it should be accepted that development of these skills in those who may be weak is likely to be a long-term challenge.
- **Interpersonal skills.** This categorization concerns those skills or behaviours which are to do with communication and may, for example, include impact, rapport–building and ability to manage confrontation. These are aspects of behaviour which are somewhat more trainable than those falling into the individual category and, as such, may be less critical to identify at the recruitment stage. None the less, if they are identified as important in the behavioural profile for the job, they should be considered when recruiting and beyond.
- **Intellectual skills.** This categorization is primarily concerned with some of the cerebral and cognitive skills relevant to the job and might include, for instance, data analysis, creativity and problem-solving.

If you are looking at managerial roles, there could be an additional section which focuses on the specific management skills and would embrace such issues as vision, empowering others and development of people.

Within this framework there would be between 60 and 100 behaviours that have already been identified as being important in the job. Each behaviour must have its own separate definition, and individuals are asked to independently assess how important that particular behaviour is in the role.

The difficulty with this approach is in identifying which behaviours should be listed and how these behaviours should be defined. If earlier research has been carried out, it is relatively easy to put together a list of behaviours that have already emerged as being of possible relevance. The only issue then is one of producing definitions. This is not as difficult as it may at first appear. To begin with, it is important to remember that these are *your* definitions and that there is no right or wrong answer. If working in a group, try brainstorming for ideas or even using a dictionary to get you started. As long as the definition is easy enough to understand it should enable the instrument to work. The most important point is that everyone works from the same definition. Wherever possible, try to provide definitions of behaviours that can be seen and ultimately measured. For example:

Initiative: Actively influences events rather than passively waiting for something to happen.

In the example above, initiative lends itself to being observed. You can identify particular activities where an individual influenced a situation rather than waiting to be told what to do. For instance, a sales executive may have decided to set up a database in order to profile and prioritize potential customers rather than continue to operate in an established way, visiting organizations on a well worn 'patch'.

It may be that your organization or function has an existing list of competencies that you can work from in constructing a Skills Analysis Questionnaire. However, if you do not have a bank of data with which to construct it, then you could work with a generic instrument, such as the Skills Analysis Questionnaire provided in Appendix 1 which you could adapt to your needs. The value in developing a Skills Analysis Questionnaire is that you start to develop language and understanding for the performance management measures that follow.

Although anybody looking at the questionnaire could, of course, argue that all the listed behaviours are important, in the briefing instructions the respondent is told that the exercise is essentially one of discrimination, and is asked to rate each behaviour as follows:

4   **Absolutely critical.** A person could not possibly perform satisfactorily in the job without a high degree of skill of this area.
3   **Essential.** It would be very difficult for a person to perform effectively in the job without considerable skill in this area.
2   **Desirable but not essential.** Skills in this area would sometimes enhance job performance, but satisfactory performance could be expected without this behaviour.

1   **Unnecessary, not required or inappropriate.** Skills in this area would almost never have anything to do with achieving success in the job.

0   **Detrimental.** Having this behaviour would actually be detrimental.

This last category raises the interesting issue that some behaviours which might be considered positive in one job role might be detrimental in another. For example, in seeking to define the behavioural profile of an air traffic controller behaviours such as risk-taking or initiative would probably be seen as dangerous whereas compliance, or following the rules, would be seen as mandatory. The reverse might be true when considering the role of, for instance, a management consultant in a small entrepreneurial business; initiative may be seen as critical and too much compliance would actually inhibit performance.

We suggest that, when rating a job role in order to produce a behavioural profile, you should aim for no more than 15 per cent of the competencies to be rated at level 4. This forces a process of discrimination which may not be easy but ensures that the really critical behaviours are identified.

In order to achieve a more reliably accurate profile there is an argument for issuing the Skills Analysis Questionnaire to all those who have an interest in, and understanding of, the job. Statistical analysis can then be used to produce the profile, based on the views of, for instance, the job-holder, the boss, direct reports and even internal customers.

Occasionally, we have designed the questionnaire to explore the behaviours in a dynamic or historic context. Here one might add a column where the respondent marks against each behaviour whether it is increasing or diminishing.

Having discussed a number of methods for defining the role let us move on to consider ways in which some of the techniques we have described were used in a real-life assignment with a major international organization.

CASE STUDY: THE CHANGING ROLE OF MARKETING AT COCA-COLA ITALIA

In 1997, following the commitment of the Italia branch of Coca-Cola to a channel marketing structure, we worked with the organization to introduce a means of assessing and developing the management team against the key requirements of their future role.

A structured process for defining the characteristics of success was adopted. It was realized early on that it was critical to understand how the role was changing and to ensure that managers were able to see how they measured up against this profile, rather than working from the basis of the job as it used to be in the old structure.

Essentially, the channel marketing structure entailed focusing organizational structures and processes around what were described as 'home' channels, which included, for instance, retail outlets, hypermarkets and supermarkets, and 'away from home' channels which included places where people might go to drink the products.

Over 50 per cent of the management population was interviewed in depth in order to discuss how the role was changing and identify the key requirements in terms of behaviours and personal skills. The following techniques were used during the interviews:

- **Diary technique** – individuals were asked to describe activities which they had engaged in during an actual working day, and the interviewers identified specific behaviours.
- **Critical incident technique** – in a similar way, interviewees described critical incidents from the recent past, and key skills and behaviours were identified.
- **Repertory grid (paired comparisons)** – interviewees were asked to compare and contrast a number of different managers they knew. In describing the differences and similarities it was again possible to see which were the key behaviours.

In addition, managers were asked to complete a Skills Analysis Questionnaire that listed over 50 personal behaviours that are often seen in an organizational context, rating these behaviours in terms of importance in the changing role of the channel marketing manager in Coca-Cola. This enabled some valuable quantitative analysis that was combined with content analysis conducted on the data from the interview techniques described above.

A behavioural profile was defined, and this detailed 32 behaviours that were grouped under the headings of Intellectual, Interpersonal, Individual and Leadership.

Intellectual behaviours were considered particularly important and comprised, for instance, visioning, strategic thinking and business awareness. In addition, interpersonal skills were becoming especially important where managers were having to define and build new channels; here, behaviours such as influencing, presenting and confronting were essential.

Certain additional individual skills were also found to be essential, and they were categorized as such because it was argued that they were more personality-related and therefore more difficult to teach; these included, for instance, initiative, the ability to make the difficult decision (which we termed 'emotional muscle') and commitment.

Once these behaviours had been agreed and defined, a questionnaire was developed, which would enable assessment of individuals against the current and future requirements of the role, and, for the whole population (that is 20 managers), assessment was conducted by themselves, their peers, their bosses and subordinates.

This led to ratings in the four categories of self, boss, peers and subordinates, and summary data was presented back to the individual managers. It was considered essential to maintain an appropriate level of confidentiality and so feedback was managed through a one-to-one discussion held between the managers and the consultants. On the basis of this, personal development plans were formulated, incorporating formal training, structured experience and coaching opportunities. In some cases, discussion led on to the identification of future potential job roles and career moves.

It can be seen in this case study that, due to the new business structure, there was a need for an objective reappraisal of job roles. Without this, managers would have been assessed against the old, and therefore inappropriate, characteristics of success. A number of interesting observations were made following the exercise. These are summarized below.

- Individual or more personality-related behaviours present more of a problem for organizations: more often there is a need to recruit people into the organization who have previously demonstrated such behaviours as they are less easy to teach or train. (How do you teach someone 'initiative' or 'commitment'?)

- In dynamic and changing environments, there is a need to review the profile of the job, rather than work on old assumptions. In the case study organization it was apparent that some managers had strong skills in terms of the old role but had clear weaknesses or development needs when assessed against the new requirements.
- Senior management commitment to the process is essential in terms of establishing credibility and support from other levels. In Coca-Cola this was not simply a human resource initiative or a consultancy assignment, it was positioned as part of a wider strategic business imperative.
- Effort needs to be put into building trust in the process. Whilst there was naturally some apprehension regarding assessment and how the data would be used, the participants in the case study were encouraged to buy into the process through close involvement in the research and regular updates regarding the project.
- It was possible to validate the results of the exercise by comparing data produced through this exercise with that produced from other sources such as performance reviews and more anecdotal data.
- Whilst most managers in Coca-Cola demonstrated a good level of self-insight – in other words, their self-review was broadly in line with that of their manager – other patterns were seen. Some, for instance, clearly had an inflated view of their own performance and ability, and this was evident where self-ratings were significantly higher than ratings of two or more other categories. Also, there were some instances where individuals had a lower opinion of their own abilities than, say, their boss, peers or subordinates; in these cases the issue of self-confidence could be addressed.

The above case study highlights certain key principles. First, as an organization, Coca-Cola was not prepared to drift into the future without spending time on seeking an answer to the question 'What will our successful people look like in the future?'. In addition, it should be noted that, although the research was thorough, the total assignment was completed in less than eight weeks.

Having formulated this profile of successful performance and having had the opportunity of looking at their current cadre of personnel, the organization was then able to put in place effective succession planning and planned training.

Summary

We have explored a number of methods for defining the critical behaviours for success in a job role. This represents the first, and arguably the most important, stage of the integrated performance management process. Ultimately, the process should lead to the formulation of a behavioural profile. In order for this profile to be useful, the number of behaviours that are listed in defining a role must be

COMPETENCE	DEFINITION
Problem analysis	Identifying problems, finding relevant information, relating data from different sources and identifying possible causes of problems
Planning	Establishing a course of action for self and/or others to accomplish a specific goal; planning proper assignments of personnel and appropriate allocation of resources
Self-organization	Ability to efficiently schedule own time and activities
Persuasiveness	Using appropriate communication skills to gain agreement or acceptance of an idea, plan, activity or product/service from others
*Initiative	Active attempts to influence events to achieve goals; self-starting rather than passive acceptance. Taking action to achieve goals beyond what is necessary; originating ideas and actions
*Decisiveness	Readiness to make decisions, render judgements, take action or commit oneself
Impact	Creating a good first impression, gaining attention and respect, demonstrating confidence
Assertive confrontation	Skill at maintaining composure and objectivity when confronted with personally defence-provoking or aggressive situations
*Energy/stamina	Maintaining a high level for long period
*Risk-taker	Taking or initiating action which involves a deliberate gamble in order to achieve a recognized benefit or advantage

Figure 2.1   Behavioural profile for the role of management consultant

limited. It can be helpful at this stage to also give thought to which behaviours are more personality-related, and therefore less trainable, and those which can be developed. In the example shown in Figure 2.1 we show the profile for the role of management consultant – a profile we have used in our own organization. As can be seen, there are certain behaviours that are marked by an asterisk; these are more innate and less trainable and therefore critical to identify at the recruitment stage.

As suggested at the start of this chapter, in order to successfully manage performance your organization needs to know precisely what is good performance in its many roles. This requires concentrating not just on the 'whats' – the outputs – but also on the 'hows' – the inputs. We have provided you with a number of pragmatic tools that we have found useful for laying down this foundation of performance management and now encourage you to consider the questions below – questions that will help you determine what actions you wish to take in your organization or team.

In the next chapter we move on to consider how to meet the challenge of recruitment. In particular, we look at how it is possible to make more effective selection decisions by using the behavioural technology we have described.

PAUSE FOR THOUGHT

- *How are jobs defined in your organization?*
- *In what way, and at what rate, are jobs changing?*
- *How is this being taken into account through organizational practices and systems?*
- *In your own role what do you consider to be the trainable behaviour requirements?*
- *What requirements do you see as less trainable and possibly more personality-related?*
- *Consider the same questions with regard to the jobs of those whom you have to manage.*
- *Which of the methods described in this chapter could you actually use more effectively in order to define roles in your organization?*

Reference

Gumesson, E. (1991), *Qualitative Methods in Management Research*, Beverly Hills, CA: Sage.

3

SELECTION

No change of circumstances can repair a defect of character.

Ralph Waldo Emerson, 1803–82
Essayist and Poet

The objectives of this chapter are as follows:

- to examine the research findings that suggest that unstructured interviews can have a low predictive validity and are generally unreliable
- to highlight the common perceptual distortions which can influence our judgements about others and which can adversely influence the selection decision
- to discuss the key competencies of an effective interviewer, using the behavioural profiling approach for defining the role, focusing on the core competencies of interviewing
- to explore the importance of understanding values and beliefs when making judgements about the fit between the individual and the organization
- to consider the issue of how to structure the interview and to provide recognized options.

In Chapters 1 and 2 we have emphasized the importance of measuring all aspects of an individual's performance, rather than focusing purely on what we described as task outputs. In our integrated and competence-based approach to performance management we now consider how you can use the behavioural profile of a role as the basis for effective selection decisions.

A prerequisite for managing performance is your organization's ability to define successful performance for the variety of roles within it. We have already considered a number of different techniques which can be used in defining successful performance. If more than one technique can be used in defining the role, then, in accordance with the principles of triangulation, the findings become more reliable and valid. Here, we move on to tackle the next stage in the model of performance management. Having defined the role as precisely as possible, we need now to consider how we recruit against that definition. Although it is assumed that you will be familiar with the basic principles of selection interviewing, we do highlight best practices so that you can compare your organization's performance in this component area of performance management.

Resourcing for results

Strategically, improving the quality of selection is likely to have a significant impact on the long-term effectiveness of any business. Often organizations fail to recognize this in their actions, although many pay lip-service to the idea. Consider, for instance, the time taken in the decision-making process when purchasing a major piece of capital equipment. Contrast this against the same time and effort taken to recruit and select a middle manager. Before we specifically look at the skills required for successful selection interviewing, let us first consider the empirical evidence that clearly demonstrates what goes wrong in selection.

Reliability and validity in selection interviewing

This issue of reliability is really about the extent to which an interview provides consistent results. For instance, does the interview give us similar results when conducted by a number of interviewers recruiting for the same role, or would two interviewers interviewing the same person come up with different results?

Overall, the evidence from research suggests that, unless the interview process is systematic, the interview tends to be unreliable: in other words, different interviewers interviewing the same person come to different conclusions and judgements. One of the key reasons for this is that the interviewers are likely to be making their assessment by interpreting information from their own unique frame of reference. One way of overcoming this difficulty is to ensure that a common description and definition of the role is agreed. This will mean using the specific tools and techniques described earlier in order to develop a robust behavioural profile.

The other measure of success, as far as the interview is concerned, is to do with validity. By this we mean the extent to which the decisions made by an interviewer are good predictors of future performance. Again, the findings, as far as unstructured and unsystematic interviews are concerned, suggest that we might as well just select names out of a hat! This may sound dramatic, but interviewers often allow a range of subjective biases to influence their thinking, and this leads to flawed decision-making.

All too often interviewers:

- base their decisions on intuition or gut feeling
- make selection decisions based on first impressions: research has shown up to 85 per cent of selection decisions are made within four minutes – indeed, research by Macan and Dipboye (1994) has shown that the impression formed even before the interview through, for instance, study of documentation, actually influences the interpretation of the applicant's behaviour during the interview
- tend to give higher ratings to traits or aspects of the interviewee responses which they can particularly relate to
- tend to make person-to-person comparisons rather than comparing each candidate to the specification identified for the role
- And finally, Baron (1989) identified that the mood of the interviewer affected their assessment of the interviewee's performance. If you are in a good mood, you will tend to rate ambiguously qualified applicants more favourably than if you are in a bad mood. If in a bad mood then you will tend to be more demanding and critical of the interviewee.

Of course, this can be countered by encouraging discipline in the use of behavioural profiles within your organization. We next explore how the profile can be most be effectively used in interviewing but, before we do this, we provide a case study showing how not to select.

CASE STUDY: THE TEN-YEAR INTERVIEW

The business was a small professional legal practice that had been established for over ten years. Essentially it was a business that consisted of four partners and it employed a trainee and qualified solicitors. It was a thriving practice that had continued to grow, albeit by a slow evolutionary process and through the development of a strong portfolio with a number of high-profile clients.

Increasingly, the partners had become worried about their capacity to deliver the level of legal services that they were being asked for, and they decided to appoint an associate partner for the practice who would have the capacity to move up to full partner status within two years. Having looked at the options internally they decided to look externally.

As this was a small business, all the existing partners felt there was a need to find someone who could be totally trusted and who could make a contribution in their own right. So it was decided to look among the existing network of people whom they had known for some time. This included friends, other similar professionals and even clients. Eventually after considerable thought and discussion, it was agreed that they would offer the opportunity to Harry who worked with a client organization in their legal department.

Harry was approaching 50 years of age, he was known to be wanting to leave his current job and look for opportunities that would allow him to continue to work for another ten years.

As far as the practice was concerned, this situation seemed ideal and was further enhanced by the fact that Harry not only had many good contacts in his industry, which could help the practice continue to grow, but he was also technically very well qualified and up to date.

The partners had known him for over ten years, they believed him to be a man of high integrity, and they knew that his personal style was such that he would probably fit well into the small 'family' culture of the practice.

No specific interview was undertaken as this seemed unnecessary, particularly given the time they had known him; however, terms of his joining and working towards partner status were agreed, and the partnership made a considerable effort to help him to make the transition.

Immediately upon appointment, however, there were warning signs of the trouble that lay ahead. First, Harry demonstrated a high degree of reliance on the existing partners for direction. On a number of occasions he asked 'What are the rules or procedures for doing this?' and was rather surprised to hear there were no rules in the sense of the strict procedures that he had become used to. Furthermore, he had a tendency to wait to be told what to do rather than taking any initiatives, and he was evidently struggling in his ability to use technology systems. It was understood that he would need some induction training and support and this was duly provided, although it soon became clear the problem was deeper than this.

Within a matter of weeks the partners were receiving complaints about Harry. Everybody agreed that he was a pleasant individual, but somehow he was described as lacking commercial drive and initiative.

The partners were clearly disappointed and had underestimated the extent to which he had become institutionalized in his previous organization. They met with Harry and explained to him the feedback they were receiving from some clients. They also expressed their concern about aspects of his self-organization and how he conducted himself in front of clients. As a result, an action plan was agreed and Harry committed to do things differently.

Things did not improve. More complaints followed and the turning point came shortly after a particular client threatened litigation following some work that Harry had carried out. By the fourth month the partners had no alternative but to end the relationship with him. It then took them almost a year, and great expense, to finally settle the severance.

On reflection afterwards, it was estimated that from his starting with the organization through to the final settlement, which was a period spanning twelve months of which he worked only four, the whole episode had cost the practice in excess of one year's salary.

What price the ten-year interview?

The above case study serves to illustrate several points. First, the partners had not sat down and defined successful performance in detail. Certainly, the ability to get on with people was important, but so were energy, stamina, decisiveness and initiative. Without these behaviours Harry was destined for failure. In fact, all of these are qualities that cannot be taught to a person in a matter of months or by sending them on a course. As discussed in Chapter 2, some of these qualities might be considered innate, and therefore untrainable, whereas others might have been developed, but over an extended period of time through a coaching process.

Also, because successful performance had not been defined, it could not be measured. Part of the problem the partners experienced in the early months was identifying exactly where he was going wrong – things didn't seem right, but it was far from clear what the problem was. Finally, in the recruiting process, they had clearly overrelied on what is often described as the 'old boy network'. In this case, what was actually more important than who Harry knew, was what he did – or, more to the point – what he did *not* do.

Now we turn our attention to what we consider to be the most important aspects of selection, showing how, if care is taken in reducing the margin for error at the recruitment stage, then all other aspects of performance management become more manageable. We describe some leading-edge approaches adopted by organizations with which we have worked in seeking to improve the reliability and validity of the selection process. This includes work completed with such organizations as Motorola, Coca-Cola and the Nestlé group. We explain how:

- focused interviewing can help overcome a number of the traditional barriers to interviewing which were described above
- focused interview questions have been formulated against organizational values in a major high-technology business
- to introduce the diary and critical incident technique as a means for identifying past behaviours
- assessment centre techniques can be used as a means of judging human potential.

As in previous chapters, you are invited to compare your own organization's performance against the features of good practice.

Selection interviews as described are fraught with problems, difficulties and misjudgements. Managers within your organization who successfully deploy the approaches described below can decrease the impact of some of these issues.

Having individuals with the right skills within your organization is critical to its success. Get selection wrong and, at best, your organization will spend its time failing to fulfil its potential whilst dealing with individual issues of under-performance.

The two main subjects covered here in detail are the use of focused interviewing and assessment centres. Linking these two approaches to selection highlights the common theme to which we have been referring throughout this book – namely, the importance of measuring behaviour and using the behavioural profile as a way of defining the skills and competencies you are looking for. Once we know what we are looking for, then a number of different assessment techniques can be deployed to identify whether an individual possesses these qualities. First, let us consider the use of focused behavioural questioning.

The focused interview

The focused interview is so described because there is a tight focus on the critical behaviours associated with success. As an approach, its value has been recognized and published by Latham (1989), who has shown that, by basing interview questions on critical incidents which differentiate between effective and ineffective performance, it is possible to achieve both higher levels of inter-interviewer reliability and a higher correlation between interviewer predictions and subsequent supervisor ratings.

As we suggested when looking at the advantages of behavioural profiling in Chapter 2, there will be some behaviours that are identified as critical and which are more difficult to train or develop in an individual. Whilst it may be rather simplistic to suggest that you either have these traits or you don't, they are certainly more difficult to acquire, often because they have been formed at an early age in a person's life. With focused questioning, it is possible to determine, with a relatively high degree of reliability, whether or not an individual has the right skill and behaviour set required for success.

Focused interviewing adopts a structured and systematic approach to gathering information about the candidate. The overall intention is to maximize the relevance and amount of information, obtained during an interview, upon which a decision about a candidate's ability to do a particular job can be made. In order to do this, the interviewer seeks information from the candidate's description of past events that demonstrates that they have previously used the required behaviour. This makes it essential that the relevant behaviours are well defined and agreed upon by all those privy to the selection process.

At the interview, the interviewer asks an initial question around a behaviour in such a way that the actual behaviour being explored is either disguised or concealed. The interviewee describes a real event from the past and the interviewer then probes to identify exactly what the interviewee's role was at the time. If the questions are sufficiently searching and the candidate is given ample opportunity to draw on real experience, then it will become obvious whether or not there is evidence of past use of the behaviour. Whilst this can be an extremely demanding approach for the interviewee, it is, in the long run, potentially more fair and accurate. Questions are guaranteed to be formulated around the requirements for the role if a behavioural profile has been produced. This prevents interviewers asking leading or inappropriate questions, based on their prejudices.

Many of the difficulties of the unstructured interview described earlier in this chapter can be overcome through the application of focused interviewing. Questions are clearly targeted on behaviours, and this assumes that all those involved in the selection process will be working on the same criteria.

The emphasis is placed on seeking evidence as to whether the relevant behaviour has been displayed or not. The most reliable predictor of future performance will be past performance. If the job role requires tenacity, for example, and the candidate provides evidence of having displayed tenacity in the past, then they are likely to be capable of displaying it in the future. The key here is evidence. Often the interviewee will answer a focused question by providing a theoretical response what might be described as the textbook answer. Such answers may provide evidence of knowledge but reveal little about experiences and behaviours. So hypothetical questions should only be used to determine an individual's knowledge or test their ability to think through a problem, rather than to seek to predict their

HYPOTHETICAL **Controlled demeanour**	FOCUSED **Controlled demeanour**
'If you were in a situation where ● your manager is away on business ● the computers go down ● the secretary is off sick ● customers are complaining about late deliveries . . . How would you cope?'	'Tell me about a situation where you have had to operate without support and without resources available, under pressure . . . ● What did you do? ● What did you feel you did well? ● What would you have better? ● How did you manage?'
Outputs	**Outputs**
Indicates knowledge (and thinking skills) as well as ability to express thoughts.	Indicates actual performance (and thinking skills) as well as ability to express thoughts and enables improved prediction of performance.

Figure 3.1   A comparison of focused hypothetical questions

future behaviour. Figure 3.1 compares a focused question with a hypothetical question around the behaviour of controlled demeanour.

One of the advantages of the focused interview strategy is that it ensures a balanced and objective approach in tackling all of the relevant behaviours, and this helps counter difficulties such as the interviewer giving too much weight to certain qualities. This also helps overcome a number of the common perceptual distortions that can hinder objectivity such as those described earlier. Assessment is made against the behavioural profile, not against other applicants and not based on the effect of perceptual distortions such as:

● **The halo or horns effect** – where one characteristic, good or bad, disproportionately colours the overall view of the candidate.
● **Attracted to like** – where we are influenced positively by those who have some similarities with ourselves, regardless of their overall merits against the requirements of the job.
● **Primacy and recency effect** – where we are disproportionately influenced by first or last impressions, which can be seen both within the interview and if we are considering a number of candidates over a period of time.

So how should managers formulate effective focused questions? Guidelines are provided below:

1 **Position the questions within the overall context of the interview.**
   The use of focused questions can appear quite intimidating for the interviewee, particularly if they have not experienced this approach before. If the interviewer simply launches into the focused interview approach without some sort of preamble or warning, the interviewee may well freeze and find

the approach overwhelming. We recommend that, when using focused interviewing, it helps to give the candidate as much warning as possible regarding the approach being adopted – possibly even at the point when the candidate is first invited to interview. This does not give any unfair advantage to the candidate as you are not actually stating which behaviours you will be questioning around, but it does allow for some mental preparation for a demanding interview. Again, at the start of the interview, it is helpful to refer to the fact that you will be using focused interviewing, and that it is not necessarily an easy process, but is designed to help you make a good assessment of the candidate's suitability for the job, which is in the interests of both parties. It may also be appropriate to ease into the focused interviewing part of the process by asking the sorts of question that the interviewee would expect to hear in any case. This will increase the 'face validity' of the interview and help the interviewee relax before increasing the level of challenge.

2   **Do not name the behaviour.**
It is preferable to omit overt disclosure of the actual behaviour for which you are seeking evidence. If you were to ask, for instance, 'Can you think of any situations in the past where you have had to display initiative?' then the sort of response you are looking for becomes rather obvious. So if you were seeking evidence of initiative you might ask the focused behavioural question in the following way: 'Can you tell me about a situation from the past where you have instigated a project or assignment right from the start?' This would allow the candidate the opportunity to provide evidence, if any exists, of having displayed the relevant competence. What you are *not* doing in this case is leading the candidate by suggesting the sort of response you would expect.

3   **Follow up the initial question with probes.**
Simply taking the first response is insufficient as far as understanding the candidate's past behaviour is concerned. There is a need to follow up with probing questions that explore exactly what the interviewee's role was. The easiest approach here is simply to keep saying 'Tell me more...', but other probing comments and questions might take the following form:

- *'Tell me what your role was in this.'* – This is a key issue, particularly when a person is describing, in response, an example of a situation or project that involved a number of people. This is likely to be the case if the person was a member of a working team or performing a managerial role. You need to unravel precisely what the person's individual contribution was. On further probing it could be revealed that the interviewee was not really the initiator but was part of a team working on a project that someone else had instigated.

- *'What did you find difficult/easy?'* – This sort of question will give you some understanding of the respondent's strengths and weaknesses, and will also reveal information on their own self-image – that is, whether they have a general tendency to see themselves in a positive or more negative light. If this question alone does not elicit much of a response, a better-quality response might be obtained by asking 'What aspects of this issue were easier than others to deal with?', which encourages the interviewee to think in relative terms.

- *'What would you do differently?'* You may also wish to ask questions in order to assess the individual's ability to intellectualize on the experience they describe to you. For some roles, this reflective ability and willingness to learn from experience is important. This is the sort of questioning which is often used in an academic tutorial environment in which students are encouraged to reflect on their own learning.

Basically, any of the open-ended questions such as those commencing with 'Why...', 'How...?', 'Tell me about...', and 'What...?' are likely to provoke a response which provides more data than the initial question alone.

4   **Challenge the hypothetical or non-specific response.**
Sometimes the respondent will respond to a focused behavioural question with a response couched in hypothetical terms – for example, 'Yes what I would do is...'. In this case the interviewer should listen to the hypothetical response, which will provide data regarding the respondent's knowledge and thinking ability, but should then follow up with 'That's interesting. Have you any actual examples of being in this sort of situation in the past?'. This should push the interviewee into drawing on a real event which provides evidence of actual past behaviour. However, if the candidate is finding it difficult to think of a real example, you may start by presenting the question as hypothetical, and then asking it again as a focused behavioural question directed towards seeking real evidence from the individual's experience.

5   **Allow time.**
Do not expect the interviewee to be able to provide an immediate response. If the candidate appears to be struggling with the approach, then allow some time and offer some support with such comments as 'I know this may be a difficult question, but take your time...'. Just because the response is not immediate does not mean that there is a lack of good evidence to be found. Sometimes the interviewee's ability to recall the event can be impaired due to the pressure of the situation. Unless quick thinking in discussion is a necessary requirement of the job, this should not count as a negative factor. You may even want to offer the candidate the opportunity to return to the question at a later stage in the interview.

Following these guidelines for asking focused behavioural questions will help overcome some of the difficulties that can be encountered, and should ultimately lead to a better quality of information on which to make judgements about a candidate's suitability for a role. As the candidate is describing real situations, you may also find that evidence is provided which is actually relevant to other, or additional, behaviours. So, for instance, the candidate who is asked a focused question seeking evidence of initiative could discuss a situation where they demonstrated other behaviours such as teamworking, persuasion, planning and organizing. These may be behaviours that have been identified on the behavioural profile as relevant, or indeed they may provide evidence of what we describe as 'contra-indicators' – particular behaviours that are actually a handicap to success in the job. So if the respondent describes a heavy dependency on rule-following and adherence to procedures, and you are seeking initiative, this might be judged as a negative quality in these circumstances.

Diary technique and critical incident analysis

In Chapter 2 we looked at how the diary or day-in-the-life technique could be used to define the key behaviours required for success in a job and how it could contribute to the development of the behavioural profile for a role. We have also seen how some organizations use exactly the same approach in order to identify the behaviours an individual has displayed in the context of selection interviewing. Here, the candidates are asked to describe activities from a recent day in their life and, as they reply, the interviewer categorizes the behaviours that are then disclosed. Again, the interviewer needs to know which behaviours to look for and, in this case, has to identify evidence of relevant behaviour from the response provided. There will also be a need to probe and to ask the interviewee to expand on particular tasks or activities that are described.

The critical incident technique works in very much the same way. The interviewee is asked to describe a specific incident that was considered 'critical' or very important in their role. This might include a difficult challenge or a problem that had to be resolved, and this is discussed in some depth through the use of probing questions. As the interviewee describes the situation, the interviewer probes in order to find out what behaviours the interviewee had to display. All the rules associated with focused questions, as discussed previously, apply.

Observable interviewee behaviours in the selection interview

There are, of course, some behaviours which can be observed in the process of the interview, and the perceptive interviewer will pick up on this evidence. For instance, at an interview it is possible to observe behaviours such as:

- impact
- rapport
- verbal skills
- communication ability
- influencing skills
- personal organization
- problem-solving.

Where these behaviours are observed, the evidence from observation can be linked with evidence from other sources such as focused questions, critical incident and the diary technique. Since, on the basis of triangulation, the likelihood of the individual displaying such behaviours, if recruited, is significantly increased, such an approach will clearly strengthen your organization's ability to place the right people in the right roles.

Focused behavioural questions around organizational values

Our exposure to many organizations in different sectors and countries has shown us that different organizations have diverse cultures and values, expressed or otherwise. If there is a clash between individual and organizational values, then, sooner or later, serious difficulties will arise and one or both parties will decide to end the relationship. This issue of compatibility of individual and organizational values has become increasingly important as organizations have recognized the benefits that come from defining, in clear terms, their own corporate values and beliefs. If the organization has moved as far as defining its key values, then seeking evidence of compatible values from the candidate can be handled through the application of focused behavioural questioning.

Exploring values

Probably the most important requirement for managers, when selecting team members, is the need to try to understand the interviewee. We believe that this understanding should be at a relatively high level rather than superficial and that it can only be achieved in the selection interview through effective questioning and probing.

A critical concept we have seen utilized in organizations that have an effective selection process is three-level questioning, as illustrated in Figure 3.2. In this figure we see that, at a basic level, questions are centred on the gathering of factual

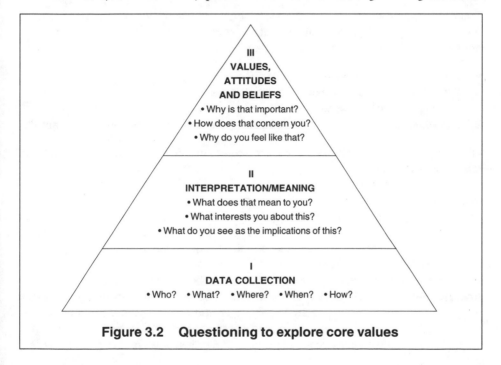

Figure 3.2   Questioning to explore core values

information. In the selection interview this may be about who the interviewee has worked for, length of employment, and size and scope of previous roles. This alone gives little true insight into the characteristics of the individual. Factually-based or level 1 questions tend to elicit level 1 responses, that is, they simply provide the database to work with. At the next level, we might ask questions about why the person worked with an organization, thereby gaining some understanding of their feeling or views. Finally, at the next level, we ask values-based or level 3 questions – questions that provide some understanding of the values or beliefs of an individual. This is the crux of the matter. If we can understand a person's values and beliefs, then we have a good indication of the 'thinking' that influences their behaviour. Remember the model shown in Chapter 1 (Figure 1.2, page 10) which showed the relationship between thinking, feeling and behaviour. If we can understand their values, then we will be able to make better informed judgements regarding how the interviewee will fit into a particular working environment.

It is this issue which is often given all too little attention in the recruitment process. How often have you seen someone join an organization to take what appears, on the face of it, to be the ideal job, only to find within a month or so that there has been a major misunderstanding and that the individual and the organization are not compatible. In order to explore this issue in more depth, we give below a real example of a questioning process in which the interviewer is seeking to understand the beliefs and values which drive the interviewee's behaviour.

EXAMPLE: VALUES-BASED QUESTIONING

The interviewer is working in a medium-sized high technology business and is seeking to recruit a manager for the telecommunications division. This organization has made an open declaration of its values, declaring that:

- Initiative and innovation are critical to our success.
- We actively seek to challenge the 'accepted wisdom'.
- We do not 'shoot the messenger' of bad news.
- Individuals are encouraged to achieve their potential through entrepreneurial activity.

(The interviewee is currently based in the telecommunications section of an international family-owned business.)

Interviewer: Can you describe your current job?

Interviewee: Certainly. I am working for Bryant Telecom. We are part of a larger family-owned business based in the north-west but operating internationally. My role is as a regional operations manager and I cover the southern region.

Interviewer: What is the size of the job in terms of budget and the team that you lead?

Interviewee: Well I currently manage a team of 30 plus. This is made up of a senior group of managers who report to me and then there are a number of supervisors, engineers and subcontractors in the structure below me. Our annual budget is in excess of 5 million and expanding gradually.

So far the interviewer has gathered some quite useful data. This, however, is only at the first level of questioning and, consequently, only provides information of a more factual nature. This is important to know, but it does not actually tell the interviewer whether there is likely to be a good fit between the interviewee and his own organization. He asks some more factual questions to satisfy himself that the relevant level of technical knowledge and experience exists, and then probes around the subject of attitudes and feelings. As we can see, this provides a higher level of information.

Interviewer: So you have been with Bryant Telecom now for five years. How do you feel about working for them?

Interviewee: Oh, I have absolutely no complaints. It is just that I feel the need to move on in my career. In truth, I really like the working environment. They are very well organized and have a good reputation in the industry. They have the backing of a larger organization and this provides some good financial stability. I have always felt my job is secure with them. What is more, there is really a family atmosphere. As you know the family are still very much involved in the business, and they offer a lot of support for their managers.

Interviewer: In what way?

Interviewee: Well there are a lot of social activities you are expected to attend as a manager, and I always meet one of the Bryants at the golf day, for instance. This provides a good opportunity to discuss business. They run a tight ship most of the time, but it is well known they are there to support you if things get tough.

Here, the interviewee is providing some information which suggests that he enjoys the security and support offered in his current organization. At this stage, the interviewer recognizes there could be some potential difficulties in terms of match. In his organization there is little support. You are very much expected to pave your own way and to break out of traditional thinking. He decides to probe further and eventually moves into third-level questioning, which confirms his suspicions.

Interviewer: So what is it about that sort of environment that makes you enjoy working in it?

Interviewee: I suppose I have always been a sociable sort of person. I work well in the team environment and that is what we have at Bryant's. This is no doubt a quality I would bring with me. I believe in giving support to others and I am good at implementing systems. Overall, I would describe myself as a good company man.

And it was this final comment which confirmed to the interviewer that there was unlikely to be a good fit. He asked a number of other questions in a different context to explore the issue of the interviewee's values and, sure enough, it was confirmed that his values were diametrically opposed to those of the business. This was not to say the interviewee was a failure – far from it. He was successful and would no doubt continue to be so in the right environment.

The interviewer walked the interviewee to the company gates and reflected on the discussion they had just had. Great qualifications and some really useful experience, but would he fit in? He noticed the candidate getting into his well polished car and carefully removing the crook-lock – a car which, incidentally, had most of the latest security gadgetry built in. He had parked in the company secure car park beneath the security office. Great attention to detail, he thought, excellent levels of compliance and evidently a meticulous person. Unfortunately, these were the opposite of the behaviours, and arguably the values, required for success in this organization; the company clearly stated that it values risk-taking, initiative and challenging of systems and procedure. 'Not a good fit' he decided.

This example underlines the importance of exploring values and beliefs. It would have been easy to fall into the trap of selecting an individual based on technical ability and the more factual data alone. By identifying the mismatch between the interviewee's values and those of the recruiting organization at the interview stage, a potentially costly recruitment mistake was avoided.

Below are some examples of focused behavioural questions that have been formulated around the values of a world's leading semiconductor organization, Xilinx. In Appendix 2 you will find a more comprehensive set of questions that were formulated for them.

Selected examples of focused behavioural questions formulated around company values

1   Customer focus

● Who do you feel are the people you have to serve most in your current role?
● How do you define their needs?
● How do you measure your performance in meeting their needs?
● How have you dealt with difficulties in meeting their needs? Give examples.

2   Respect

● Can you think of a situation where you have worked with someone who has a different style to yourself?
● Describe how you differed.
● How did you manage the difference in styles?

3   Excellence

● What personal goals and targets have you set for yourself in the past?
● How have you approached working towards these goals?
● What has been your progress?
● How have you handled difficulties or setbacks?

4   *Accountability*

● Where have you had experience of leading or managing others?
● What were the challenges/difficulties?
● How did you manage these?
● How did you assign tasks?
● How did you let people know how they were doing?

5   *Teamwork*

● When have you had to go along with a group activity that is of no real personal interest?
● How did you cope with this?

6   *Integrity*

● Give an example of where you have felt compelled to adjust the rules according to the circumstances or situation.
● What sort of standards (social, ethical and organizational) do you set?
● When have these been challenged?
● How did you manage the situation?

7   *Very open communication*

● Consider a situation where you have been criticized or given negative feedback. What was the criticism?
● How valid do you feel it was?
● How did you handle it?
● Are you ever privy to information which you feel should be withheld from others? Give examples.
● What determines who does get given the information and who does not?

Next, we look at the role of assessment centres in selection. These might incorporate all the techniques described so far in this chapter, but also provide the opportunity for the deployment of a range of other methods.

Assessment centres

The advantage of behavioural interviewing in the selection process is that it is relatively cost-effective. The main costs associated with such an approach are those related to the training and development of the relevant skills amongst those who are involved in the process. Beyond that, there is the time taken for preparation and the actual interviewing. There are more sophisticated approaches to selection, and for some time assessment centres have been used as a means of systematically assessing groups of candidates. Such an approach, if managed properly, can be very powerful and can provide an even more reliable indicator of future behaviours. In theory, assessment centres increase the validity of your decisions through triangulation since they use a variety of techniques to determine abilities. The advantage of the assessment centre approach is that you have an opportunity to see the candidate in a number of different situations, handling various tasks and challenges. It also offers a good opportunity to triangulate the findings regarding a candidate's profile, as data could be drawn from, for instance, group discussions, interviews and psychometric tests. Furthermore, because a number of assessors are usually involved in the assessment process, if they are managed correctly and are working against a commonly understood behavioural profile, the level of objectivity is increased.

So what are the sorts of exercise that might be incorporated into an assessment centre? There are many, and we will now discuss some of the more commonly used techniques.

First it should be recognized that the *focused interview* actually has a place in the assessment centre itself. Whilst the focused interview provides information regarding the candidate's experience and behaviour from the past, most of the exercises described below provide evidence of current behaviours. Using both allows a useful comparison between the candidate's account of their past experiences and observed behaviour, and moreover allows the assessors to focus in on any particular areas of concern that may have been highlighted through the focused interview.

Beyond the focused interview, the purpose of exercises used in assessment centres is to try to re-create situations that match closely with the demands of the job, on the principle that this is as close as possible to actually giving the person the job and assessing them in practice.

A frequently used exercise for those seeking managerial jobs is the *'in-tray' exercise*. Here, the candidates are provided with an in-tray full of the sorts of document that they might encounter in the job if appointed, and they are asked to work through it, marking up the actions they would take in respect of each item. This allows the assessors to identify the candidate's approach to problem-solving, prioritizing and decision-making. If using this approach, you should always check that the correct behaviours required for the job are being assessed – will the job-holder actually have to display prioritization, problem-solving and decision-making? Such an approach will also reveal whether a candidate has the relevant level of technical knowledge required.

Another advantage of the assessment centre approach is that it affords the opportunity for group interaction, as normally a number of candidates will attend at the same time. It is common to include, for instance, a *group discussion* in which the candidates are required to hold a simulated 'meeting' in order to discuss a range of job-related issues. Again, the advantage here is that realistic topics can be identified and real behaviours can be observed as the candidates hold the meeting. Typically, the 'fishbowl' approach will be used where the assessors sit outside of the group to observe particular candidates, and record evidence of the behaviours specified in the behavioural profile.

In a similar way, candidates are sometimes asked to prepare and make a *presentation*. This is a good way of assessing candidates' presentation skills and technical understanding of a subject, but, again, the key question is 'Are presentation skills critical to success in the role?'.

In just the same way, if written skills are seen as critical in the job, then the candidates may be required to carry out a *written exercise*, for instance, a technical translation or summarizing documents. Subsequently, their work will be assessed against criteria such as accuracy, speed and technical knowledge.

Role-plays can be used as a way of examining the repertoire of interpersonal skills a candidate might possess. These can be designed in order to test specific skills such as assertiveness, influencing or sales ability. Of course, it should be recognized that role-plays are not a direct replication of reality and there may be an element of acting displayed; however, if the assessor is working with a behavioural profile, then the role-play approach can clearly reveal individuals' interpersonal strengths and weaknesses.

Often, a range of written *tests* are conducted as a key component of the assessment centre, and these might take many forms. You should take care not to administer tests just for the sake of it, and it is essential to identify specifically what you are trying to achieve before deciding what sort of test to use. Although they have become more popular in recent years, tests have, in some cases, had a bad press because the following guidelines have not been followed:

- Assessors should be very clear about what they are trying to measure.
- The tests should be administered by professionals who are trained to the correct standards.
- Tests should not have built-in bias (for instance, gender or racial).
- Candidates should be briefed clearly regarding the purpose of testing.
- Feedback should be provided regarding the results.
- Tests should be used in conjunction with other methods of assessment.

Essentially, tests fall into two categories – those of mental and physical ability. There are many tests available which try to measure mental ability but, as we discussed earlier, the nature of intelligence is subject to a range of definitions and we need to be aware of the danger of assessing against the wrong criteria. Mental ability tests may assess knowledge of, say, literacy or numerical ability or professional knowledge. Aptitude tests try to assess whether an individual will have the ability to develop the relevant skills for the job were they to be given training. Physical ability tests focus more on requirements, such as manual dexterity or to detect colour blindness, which are important issues for certain occupations.

Overall, it has been found that the use of tests can significantly increase the selector's ability to anticipate future work performance, although the caveats outlined above, in terms of how tests are administered, are critical.

Mention should be made here of the use of *personality profiling* instruments, as these often feature in the design of assessment centres. Basically, personality profiling instruments try to assess the more stable personality-related traits that we display. There are many theories of personality, and it is fair to say that none has any definitive answers regarding the composition of personality. Most instruments attempt to measure certain personality-related traits, often across a range such as extroversion–introversion and dominance–compliance. Some instruments are much more complex than others, but the same objective tends to apply:

the aim is to plot where an individual tends to operate against the relevant person-ality-related dimensions or traits, through the scoring of an instrument. A key question to ask when considering the use of personality profiling instruments is how valid and reliable they are – that is, to what extent they have been proven to measure what they claim to measure, and to what extent the results obtained would be consistent if the individual were to complete the instrument again. Reputable instruments will have evidence of strong validity and reliability against high norms – in other words, many people who have completed the instrument and contributed to the evidence. None, however, is 100 per cent valid and reliable and, as there is always a margin of error, the results should be seen in the wider context of other assessment methods.

Nevertheless, personality profiling can prove very useful in identifying whether a person has certain traits that are definitely likely to inhibit success in a role. For instance, while high levels of creativity and independence would be counterpro-ductive in an air traffic controller, such qualities might be absolutely essential for a marketing executive in a small entrepreneurial business. Personality profiling can have the advantage of allowing the recruiter to seek evidence of those traits which may have been identified from the behavioural profile as essential, but more diffi-cult to develop or train. As we have already suggested, you need to bring in people from outside the organization who have the relevant innate behaviours.

Case studies have a place in the assessment centre, and these are best developed around real business situations. A real scenario from the past, which involves a number of decisions to be made, is outlined and, as the candidates work with the case, they describe what they would do and what their thinking is at each stage. This can provide insight into a range of skill areas such as the level of thinking, strategic problem-solving, technical knowledge, analytical ability and creativity.

Finally, the assessment centre, because it is normally conducted over a period of at least one day, allows for a degree of *informal observation*. This means that even though the candidates are likely to be trying to present themselves in the best possible light, and impressions management may come into play, there is more of an opportunity to observe real behaviour than in the interview alone.

Summary

We have described the weaknesses of 'traditional' interviews and the importance of enhancing the validity and reliability of selection within your organization through the use of focused questioning. We have looked at how some organiza-tions are using this approach to ensure that those people they recruit are compat-ible with the organizational values and will fit into the organization. In addition, we have explored the use of assessment centre techniques in order to increase the chances of getting it right. Even if you are a seasoned campaigner in terms of recruitment experience, you should ask yourself whether you apply sound methods in identifying whether potential candidates will display the required behaviours according to the behavioural profile. In particular, do you work hard at seeking evidence of those behaviours that are difficult to develop or assess? And if you are considering the subject from a senior human resource management role you might consider the effectiveness of your managers in using the techniques described here.

PAUSE FOR THOUGHT

- *How effective is the use of focused questions in your organization?*
- *How could recruitment processes be developed to incorporate focused interviewing techniques?*
- *Take your organization's stated values and consider the sorts of behaviour you would expect people who work to these values to display.*
- *How do you currently seek compatibility between organizational and individual values in selecting?*
- *What criteria are used for selecting people in your organization?*
- *How much attention is given to behaviour, as distinct from technical ability, in selection?*

References

Baron, R.A. (1989), 'Impression Management by Applicants During Employment Interviews: The "Too Much of a Good Thing Effect"', in R.W. Eder and G.R. Ferris (eds), *The Employment Interview: Theory, Research and Practice*, Newbury Park, CA: Sage.

Latham, G.P. (1989), 'The Reliability, Validity and Practicality of the Situational Interview' in in R.W. Eder and G.R. Ferris (eds), *The Employment Interview: Theory, Research and Practice*, Newbury Park, CA: Sage.

Macan, T.H. and Dipboye, R.L. (1994), 'The Effects of the Application on Processing of Information from the Employment Interview', *Journal of Applied Social Psychology*.

4

COACHING

One must learn by doing the thing: for though you think you know it, You have no certainty, until you try.

Sophocles, *c.* 496–406 BC

The objectives of this chapter are as follows:

- to provide an understanding of objective methods for determining developmental needs
- to explore the characteristics of how we learn and some of the barriers to effective learning
- to explain an approach to coaching that can be used in order to improve performance in the current role
- to consider the role of coaching in supporting a performance management strategy and to identify key coaching competencies
- to discuss a range of approaches that can be taken in order to exploit opportunities for learning and personal development
- to explore ways of improving motivation by looking at how one's self-concept is developed and can be challenged.

In Chapter 3 we introduced methods for enhancement of objectivity in the selection of people. This approach built on the ideas of determining roles by using behavioural competencies as the basis for any performance management system. Previously we argued that effective performance management requires a clear understanding of what good performance in a role 'looks like'.

We now move on to consider the next stage in the model of performance management, coaching. Coaching is primarily to do with the question of how we can help others to improve in their current role. This chapter describes leading-edge practices and understanding in the area of employee coaching and is based on work we have conducted with organizations such as Allied Domecq and Lotus Development, the software organization.

Whilst the approach we describe here does incorporate a number of tools and techniques to support the coaching process we would argue that coaching is more than just this. In a sense, the challenge for the human resources or organizational development professional is to help the organization to move towards a coaching philosophy of leadership. Obviously, this means providing training and appreciation of the tools and techniques, but it also means being able to recognize the qualities of an effective coach and being seen to reward strong coaching behaviour throughout the organization.

Understanding learning and change

In order to be able to understand the coaching process it is first important to have a practical appreciation of the psychology of change and learning. We hold a fundamental view that learning and change are synonymous. We assert that real learning is about personal change. This change takes place at the individual and organizational level and results in different ways of perceiving and behaving.

As can be seen in Figure 4.1, we suggest that learning takes place at four ascending levels. At a basic level, knowledge can be acquired and, beyond that, the skills or ability to implement certain knowledge might be implemented. It is beyond this level, however, that learning or change becomes especially challenging. The third stage is to do with motivation and, in our experience, although people may acquire new knowledge and develop new skills, this does not necessarily mean they are willing to implement such new skills in the real-world. Furthermore, we would go as far as to say that they might have the motivation, but they fail to make the transition at the fourth level of implementation or

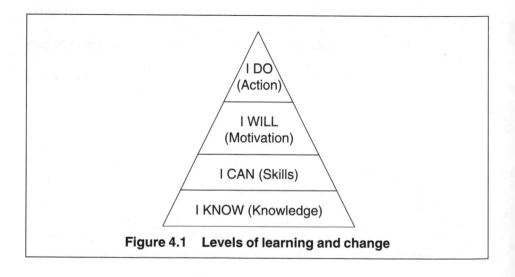

Figure 4.1   Levels of learning and change

'I do'. Learning – real learning – we assert, starts when an individual, or indeed an organization, applies its knowledge, skills and motivation in order to change.

We have increasingly come to the conclusion that, in order to enable individuals to progress successfully through to the 'I do' stage of learning or change, there is a need to provide more than just off-the-job training courses or formal management education. One of the most powerful methods is to use real-life learning opportunities that exist in the job and organization by taking a structured approach to coaching.

Coaching is essentially about how to maximize individual performance in the current role and how to promote and support an individual's learning. The benefits of achieving this for your organization are considerable and are described by Stata (1989) who suggests that an organization's only source of competitive advantage is its ability to learn. Consider, for a moment, the answers to these two simple questions:

1   What are the characteristics of an organization or team that is learning?
2   What are the characteristics of an organization or team that is not learning?

We have used these questions with groups when exploring the question 'Why coach?' The answers provide valuable insights into why an organization or a team needs to promote learning

Typically, answers to the first question include: higher morale, increased productivity, improved customer satisfaction, a higher share price, increased innovation and lower absence levels. Answers to the second question naturally cover the opposite. Comparison of the answers to these two questions provides compelling evidence for investing in performance management. It is also thought-provoking, if one was to score the organization described in answer to the first question as a 10 and that described by the second as a 0, to rate the effectiveness of your own organization in supporting learning and change.

More recently, coaching skills have been recognized as an important aspect of the managerial skill-set. The case for coaching is now as strong as it has ever been, given the accelerating rate of change and the need to constantly seek ever more effective working practices.

To help your organization maximize the potential contribution of its employees through the use of coaching we first explore how adults learn. Such knowledge and understanding is fundamental to managers who coach and get work done through others.

How do adults learn?

In many ways the issue of adult learning is far from simple. First, as adults, we have already a vast bank of previous learning to call upon and although this might initially seem to be an advantage there are potential downsides. One of the main barriers here is the problem of what we call 'unlearning'. In other words, when confronted by the challenge of having to do things differently we are often inhibited by years of experience of doing things in a certain way. An obvious example here is the use of technology. Hardly an industry or job role can claim to have been unaffected by developments in technology in recent years, yet people often resist the take-up of new technological 'tools'. If an individual has learned to succeed in the past without the need for computer technology, then why change? Being expected to carry out one's role in a different way, using new tools and techniques is likely to feel most uncomfortable, and the discomfort will be exacerbated by the strength of prior learning.

This means that an important aspect of performance and change management is the need to help others to unlearn old ways and move outside their comfort zone, to do things differently. This is probably one of the biggest challenges of performance management, and we have seen many examples of organizations deciding at the top level how things should be done and making a declaration to those who are expected to change. It is often assumed that, by simply stating the new thinking, new behaviours or even new beliefs and values which a select few have decided upon, people will be able adopt new ways of behaving and thinking. In reality, very little changes by simply making the statement; people must be helped through the change process and should be given support in facing the need for learning and unlearning.

Figure 4.2 shows a model described as the stages of learning. This shows that, before many learning processes begin, we are in a state of unconscious incompetence. This is really the state of not knowing what we do not know or 'ignorance is bliss'. This 'state' is presented in a humorous way in a Calvin and

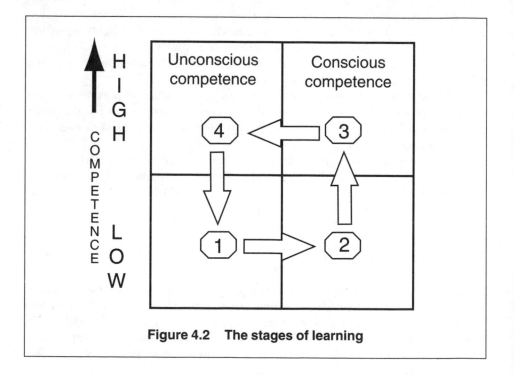

Figure 4.2   The stages of learning

Hobbes cartoon sequence. This cartoon shows Calvin and Hobbes riding a push-cart. They declare how blissful ignorance is and how happiness can be maintained through stupid short-term self-interest. As they push their cart towards a cliff edge, Calvin says 'We're heading for that cliff!' Hobbes' response is 'I don't want to know about it'. After plunging over the cliff Calvin says, 'I'm not sure I can stand so much bliss' to which Hobbes replies, 'Careful! We don't want to learn anything from this'.

Let us look at the model of the hierarchy of learning with regard to the example of the use of technology as described earlier. An individual may not know how technology could be used and not knowing may feel all right. Often at this stage people will actually deny the need to know any more than they currently do and resist the persuasive attempts of others to encourage them to learn. However, if they do break out of the state of unconscious incompetence then it is most likely that the next stage will be a state of conscious incompetence. This is the stage at which we start to realize how much we do not know and this clearly can be frightening. It is the stage where, for example, the person adopting a new computer system, turns to the first page of the manual only to read in the introduction that, in order to have an elementary command of the system, there is a requirement to become familiar with a minimum of 300 basic commands! At this point many people actually decide to quit the learning process because the whole idea of continuing seems too daunting. In order to persevere, therefore, they need a great deal of encouragement and support. One British manager who was required by his employer to learn French to an effective business level described rather well the approach his French tutor took to help him through the psychological barrier. He was told that he needed to develop a basic vocabulary of 2000 words which at first sounded impossible until he was then informed that he already had a knowledge of at least 500 French words which are actually used in the English language. In terms of confidence this helped him immensely in approaching the learning process. This takes us to stage two in the model, in which motivation and the need to build the learner's confidence are the priority.

If the learner does persevere, then the next stage to be experienced is where competence increases accompanied by a heightened consciousness of doing things differently. This is where the new skills or behaviours are being applied but in a very self-conscious way. Consider the process of learning to drive: at the outset the learner is often taught a routine to remember such as 'mirror, signal, manoeuvre'. Initially the learner makes a very conscious effort to ensure that this procedure is followed on every occasion. Eventually, however, as the level of learning increases the new skill becomes more embedded in the individual's behaviour and it is carried out without conscious thought. This stage might be described as unconscious competence and is the goal in terms of learning. A word of caution, though. To return to the analogy of learning to drive, when people have been driving for a long time they frequently fall into bad habits without realizing it, while in fact considering themselves as particularly good drivers. The model suggests, then, that learning should be viewed as more of a continuous process than one with a beginning and an ending. In supporting the learning process at stage three – conscious competence – there is a need for encouragement, support and feedback, and as learning progresses to stage four there will be less need for direct feedback as the learner starts to integrate new skills into their repertoire of behaviour.

An awareness of the hierarchy of learning can provide some comfort to those learners who may be experiencing the pain associated with, say, stage two and the self-consciousness of stage three. Equally, it should be reassuring to the coaches who might be feeling the frustration associated with guiding a coachee through the hierarchy.

Another useful model of learning has been developed by Honey and Mumford (1992), who, building on the work of Kolb (1984), suggest that, in terms of how we learn, we have particular preferences, referred to as our learning styles. It is suggested that there are four types of learning style: Activist, Reflector, Theorist and Pragmatist; and that these four learning styles relate to the four stages of the experiential learning cycle – experience, reviewing, concluding and planning. A major contribution of this model has been to encourage recognition of the fact that we all can learn in a variety of ways but, because of our own learning style preferences, we will feel more comfortable with some approaches to learning than others.

A strong Activist learning style is associated with learning by doing, action and risk-taking. Activists will respond well to being thrown in at the deep end and being given projects and assignments to push them outside their comfort zone.

Reflectors tend to stand back, take a more conservative approach, think things through beforehand and reflect on the experience afterwards. They tend to collect and analyse data from a number of perspectives. A more cautious approach is required in developing a Reflector, who would feel less comfortable being pushed into higher-risk situations.

Those with a preference for the Theorist style of learning tend to want to understand how things work and have a strong need to get beneath the surface to understand basic principles and assumptions. In developing the Theorist there will be more need to provide theoretical underpinning and to appeal to logic.

Finally, the Pragmatist learning style is associated with trying out new ideas and techniques rather than spending too long thinking things through. As far as the development of the Pragmatist is concerned there is a need to help them develop plans and to provide new experiences to experiment with.

Clearly, there is a danger in overgeneralizing and it should be stated that we all have the ability to learn in all four ways – we are only talking about *preferences* here. In managing the performance of others it can be helpful to recognize preferred learning styles not simply because this will help in deciding how to provide training and development, but also because the learning style framework relates, in many ways, to broader personality styles and, as such, gives some indication of how people are likely to prefer to be managed or coached.

The increasing interest in the subject of learning in recent years is, in many ways, a reflection of the increasing rate of change which many organizations and industries have had to confront. Without the ability to refer to a body of knowledge on how something should be done – because it is often being done for the first time – the individual has to become increasingly comfortable with the concept of learning by doing. Furthermore, those providing managerial education have now realized that learning is often more effective when it is facilitated and explored in the real work situation.

Following the principles of action learning as propounded by the likes of Revans as far back as the 1940s it is now possible to follow an MBA or doctoral level research qualification by working with other managers in sets which may be geographically spread over the globe. Using the technology of the Internet and the concept of the virtual university this is now possible through organizations such as International Management Centres.

Also, in recent years, many organizations and researchers have suggested the aspirational concept of the learning organization whereby the organization learns through the continual learning of its members. Naturally, for such aspirations to become reality individuals must have a healthy learning orientation, and it is worth considering an individual's learning orientation level and the level at which they should be operating. At a basic level, learning orientation is about seeking improvements to existing procedures and seeking feedback in order to learn lessons that will facilitate improvements in the future. Those learning at this level will:

- look at past successes and difficulties to see what went right and to avoid what went wrong
- seek to improve performance
- react positively when faced with mistakes or development needs
- encourage subordinates to try new ways of working
- demonstrate belief in personal development.

At the next level, effective learning orientation is about seizing developmental opportunities and using experiences to improve personal and business performance. Those operating at this level will:

- take opportunities to learn and initiatives to gain feedback
- identify their own strengths and weaknesses from previous experiences
- identify personal and team development objectives
- orchestrate developmental experiences and assignments
- facilitate the sharing of learning and best practices.

Then, at the advanced level, a strong learning orientation is seen where the individual actively and overtly identifies lessons learnt and shares plans to apply these in future activities. At this level the individual:

- sets clear objectives against which to measure personal performance
- actively learns from their own personal successes and failures as well as their own observations and analysis of others' experiences
- admits responsibility for mistakes or contributions to problems and openly seeks advice on ways to avoid these or improve in future
- positively seeks or constructs learning and feedback opportunities

- displays an open management style which is receptive to new ideas and approaches.

By briefly looking at the three models related to the learning process, we suggest that the manager, as coach, would benefit from:

- recognizing the learner's position on the hierarchy of learning
- understanding the learner's and their own learning style preferences

and

- considering the individual's learning orientation.

These models are presented as a useful backdrop because coaching is essentially about supporting a process of individual learning and change. We now move on to explain the model of coaching that we work with, and the associated tools and techniques. This coaching model is based on best practice and, in particular, our experience in implementing a global coaching programme for over 300 managers within the drinks giant Allied Domecq and in the European division of Lotus Development, the software organization.

The role of coaching

We define coaching in the following ways:

- a way of getting people to perform to the best of their ability in their current role
- the process of identifying and using opportunities at work as a vehicle for guided learning
- improving knowledge and skill both formally and informally.

Incorporated into these definitions there are a number of important concepts which should be highlighted. First, coaching is about improving performance in the current role; it is not a one-off event or something that the manager, as coach, does at a fixed time each week. More often it is part and parcel of the relationship which unfolds over time – indeed, some organizations have described coaching as a leadership philosophy to which they aspire. In stating that it is about getting people to perform to the best of their ability in their current role we are making a case that coaching is relevant for most managers. If you feel that all your team members are currently performing to the best of their ability, then maybe you are already carrying out effective coaching or you do not need to. But how many managers could, hand on heart, say this is so?

Furthermore, we place the emphasis on the current job role because we believe that coaching is more often related to the here and now of the current job rather than the future. By contrast, mentoring, which is described in detail in Chapter 6, is concerned more with the development of the individual beyond the current role.

Coaching is based in the work environment, not normally the classroom, and is about seeking to identify opportunities in the job role to enhance individual learning and improvement. Finally, we recognize that coaching can be both an informal and a formal process. It is often the case, for instance, that peers coach peers and subordinates may even informally coach their managers or supervisors.

Many organizations have come to recognize the value of coaching and, at an organizational level, the benefits are many. Ultimately, coaching is about creating and exploiting the opportunity for development in the work environment. It is real; the individual spends less time away from the job and more time developing skills in the practical work environment. Building the skills and a culture of coaching can help the organization at a corporate level to integrate its broader human resource strategy. At Allied Domecq Spirits and Wine, for instance, a major international coaching programme forms part of the broader performance management system, and it is clearly linked to processes and systems. At the start of any coaching programme a senior manager will make a presentation reinforcing messages regarding the performance management system including, for example, resourcing, performance appraisal and remuneration. At the level of the individual manager there are, again, benefits to accrue through adopting a coaching approach to management, such as improved personal relations and, by delegating more to the coachee, freeing time to spend on critical activities. For the individual being coached there are opportunities to build confidence, to develop problem-solving skills, to ensure a better understanding of what is expected and to learn to cope with change. However, coaching should not simply be seen as a stand-alone technique; it is an ongoing process which entails a number of key steps. Moreover, associated with these steps are a number of key skills which need to be displayed and a range of techniques which can be deployed.

Figure 4.3 shows a model of coaching which we have developed, based on

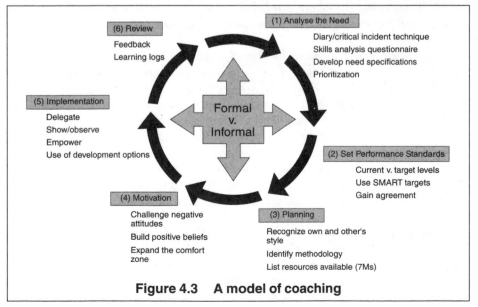

Figure 4.3   A model of coaching

observation and our own experiences of coaching both within our own and client organizations. This process, which entails a number of key stages and associated techniques should be seen as a conceptual and practical guide rather than a rigid template. We advocate the adoption of this model into an organization's performance management strategy and outline a developmental programme designed to enhance coaching competence. At a personal level, if you are involved in coaching others you may be able to identify where in the model you currently are, although it should be recognized that the process is not necessarily sequential. However, let us now work through the stages and techniques of the model.

Stage 1: Analyse the need

Determining an individual's real developmental needs is the critical first step. A number of specific techniques might be deployed in order to determine the key needs of the 'coachee'. At a basic level, observation may lead to the obvious identification of a development need which might be addressed through coaching. However, in many job roles, it is not possible to shadow a person and observe everything they are doing in order to identify their areas for development. So a variety of interview techniques might be deployed.

As discussed in Chapter 2, the use of diagnostic techniques, such as the diary technique and critical incident analysis, can help identify development needs. In applying these techniques in this context the initial step would be to ask the coachee to describe their activities of, say, the previous day. These would be probed in detail in order to explore the specific skills and behaviour which were required and to find out how the individual coped. By then asking about specific critical incidents or situations it is possible to further explore issues of performance and difficulty. By asking about what was done, how it was done and what were the real difficulties, it is possible to eventually identify the person's development needs.

If a behavioural profile exists for the job role, this would form a good basis for identifying development needs. You would work from the critical behaviours and explore the extent to which the person has been able to use the required skills. A particularly structured approach could involve the use of the Skills Analysis Questionnaire as shown in Appendix 1. This approach was discussed in Chapter 2 where we showed how the questionnaire can be used to help profile the requirements for the job. To identify personal development needs, the profile would be used to determine how the individual is performing against, in particular, those skills and behaviours rated as critical or '4'. In the spirit of coaching it would be appropriate for the coachee to complete such a questionnaire and then to compare their self-ratings with those of the manager or coach.

Other techniques which can be used during this identification stage include the Development Need Specification and the prioritization of development needs. The Development Need Specification uses a process of discussing what the need is and what the need is not, using the format shown in Figure 4.4.

This approach to identifying development need helps to provide focus by

	The Development Need is . . .	The Development Need is not . . .
Who		
Where		
When		
What		
How shown		

Figure 4.4   Development Need Specification

	The Development Need is . . .	The Development Need is not . . .
Who	James Barter	
Where	Project X	Project Y (yet) though could be in 3 months' time.
When	When working with senior engineers.	
What	Confidence in taking on new assignments. Meetings and presentation skills.	Technical skills – these are strong. Supervisory skills – though could be in future.
How shown	Hesitant in making recommendations in meetings.	

Figure 4.5   Development Need Specification: worked example

distinguishing between where there is a need and where there is not. So, for instance, the development needs for a new graduate recruited into a team of engineers might present as illustrated in Figure 4.5.

A prioritization of needs might also be necessary, particularly if a number of development needs are apparent, and the approach shown in Figure 4.6 could help in this respect. With this approach we are seeking to distinguish between those development needs which might be considered urgent and those development needs which are serious. In other words, there will be some needs which are serious but may not be burningly urgent and, as such, they need to be considered. Then there is the issue of growth. What we are trying to discover here is to what extent the development need will grow if nothing is done about it. First, a

	Development need		
Seriousness			
Urgency			
Growth			
Totals			

Figure 4.6   Prioritizing development needs

	Development need		
	Presentation skills	Supervisory management	Bid preparation
Seriousness	6	4	4
Urgency	4	2	8
Growth	7	8	5
Totals	17	14	17

Figure 4.7   Prioritizing development needs: worked example

quantifiable measure is decided – say, on a scale of 1 to 10. Then, continuing with the example of James Barter, the graduate engineer, the prioritization might look something like that in Figure 4.7.

From Figure 4.7 we can see here that supervisory skills are important in the long term, (assuming James decides to follow a managerial career path) and will grow into a big problem. However, this is not really a matter of urgency at the current time. By contrast it, can be seen that being able to prepare bids is an urgent issue due to the current workload but this is not so serious a matter in the whole scheme of things. In this particular case, presentation skills and bid preparation would probably be given the more immediate attention, whilst recognizing the need to provide supervisory training and development in the future.

Essentially what we are describing in these techniques is the need to work with an analytical structure in order to ensure that the real development needs are identified. It is only once we have understood the development need for the coachee that we can move into establishing standards and targets in a focused way.

Stage 2: Set performance standards

Having identified as clearly as possible the individual's develo[p]
next stage is to identify and establish performance standards or ta[rgets]
niques here are target setting as discussed next in Chapter 5[.]
coachee in formulating his or her own targets is important at this ....g.. as one of
the aims in setting up a coaching relationship is the need to create a feeling of
involvement and therefore ownership. The principles of SMART targets which
are discussed in detail in the context of performance review in Chapter 5, are
valuable here – namely, that targets should be:

- Specific
- Measurable
- Achievable and acceptable
- Realistic and relevant
- Time-bound.

In many organizations target setting is built formally into the performance
appraisal process and there will be organizationally defined guidelines on how to
set targets. Increasingly, organizations have recognized the need to set targets that
address behavioural inputs, rather than simply performance outputs such as profits, service levels or production. Companies talk of developmental targets or a
process of personal development planning. Whether or not target setting is formally built into the organization's performance management process and procedures, there is a strong case for ensuring that targets are set to provide goals
for the individual to aim for in improving ability in the current role, as per our
original definition of coaching.

One criticism of the way in which some target setting exercises are implemented is that the emphasis is often exclusively placed on what the individual has to do
or achieve. Sometimes this is to the exclusion of any overt statement of what the
individual's manager will do to help support their progression towards achieving
the target. In the context of coaching we would argue that the manager, as coach,
should demonstrate some commitment to support the coachee – for example, by
offering time or other resources to support learning and development.

More details of the target setting process are given in Chapter 5 and in Hale and
Whitlam's *Target Setting and Goal Achievement* (1997). The key point at this
stage, however, is to recognize that target setting must be agreed before individuals are expected to work towards their achievement and that they should be related to the identified gap between current and required performance levels, as
clarified at stage 1.

Once targets have been set jointly it will be easier for the coach and coachee to
consider how to work towards meeting the need. This brings us to stage 3 in the
coaching cycle, planning.

Stage 3: Planning

Planning learning as part of a coaching strategy should entail consideration of both learning styles and methods. We have already discussed learning styles and how different people will have their own unique preferences. If someone has a highly Activist and Pragmatic preference they will probably feel more comfortable if you use active methods of development – for example, they will respond well to being given special projects and assignments and being expected to take the initiative. If anything, they may need your support in helping them consolidate their learning and reflect on it after the event.

By contrast, those with Reflector and Theorist preferences will respond well to learning events which are well thought through in advance and where the relationships with theoretical concepts are clear. In this case the coach will need to help in making such connections, whilst at the same time encouraging spontaneity.

Considering the style of the coachee, however, only addresses part of the problem in planning coaching interventions. A good coach will recognize the influence of their own preferred learning style and will be sensitive enough to know that what appeals to him- or herself may not necessarily appeal to the coachee. Equally, it could also be argued that if the coach has a different style, the two contrasting styles of the coach and coachee may possibly complement each other. This is a compelling argument, as we know that people with contrasting styles often work well together, but the secret is to be aware of the styles issue and be committed to using it as a strength.

Having considered learning styles, the coach will need to identify the methods of learning; here, there are many options other than the obvious one of sending the individual on a training course. For instance, could the role be enriched by delegating more or simply enlarged through the assignment of additional responsibilities? Could the coach provide structured guidance in conveying new skills or knowledge? What about a special assignment where the coachee is expected to take full responsibility for a particular project which will necessitate the deployment of new skills? Thinking creatively, could the coachee temporarily take on a different role in order to broaden experience or see things from a different perspective? Could the coachee be assigned as the understudy or protégé to another person who has strong knowledge and skills? Is mentoring appropriate and who would make a suitable match? Are there materials which can be made available in order to develop managerial or technical skills? What about asking the coachee to lead a particular meeting or presentation, or head up a task force or project team? How about conferences or workshops in order to broaden knowledge skills and networks?

A useful categorization at this stage of planning development is to consider the use of the 7Ms as a way of identifying the resources which could be made available. These are:

- Machines   Could equipment or capital items be made available?
- Money   Are there budgets or financial resources to offer?
- Minutes   What about time commitment from the coach and coachee?

- Manpower   Are there human resource considerations?
- Materials   Are there any materials that the coachee could draw on?
- Market   Are there any (internal or external) market considerations?
- Methods   Could methods of operating be developed or changed?

In Appendix 6 we have taken each of the competencies described in the Skills Analysis Questionnaire (Appendix 1) and have built on our understanding of what good and not so good behaviour against these competencies specifically looks like and then included ideas regarding development options. We believe that considering such a broad range of methods should help deter the all too common 'training course' mentality where, at the first sign of a development need, the manager reaches for the training course directory.

Stage 4: Motivation

So far, in the model of coaching, we have considered a number of the tools and techniques that can be used in order to identify the need, set targets for and plan personal development. With our recommended emphasis on considering these issues from a behavioural perspective we have been suggesting a more analytical and defensible approach to people development. But what happens when we are doing all these things right as a coach and, for some reason that is difficult to pinpoint, the coachee is failing to make the transition described at the start of this chapter from knowledge and skills into motivation and action?

This leads us to now consider the challenge of motivation. Often managers describe motivation as the most difficult aspect of coaching and we would support this thesis.

Referring back to Figure 4.1 and the different levels of learning and change we see that, at a basic level, people acquire knowledge. From an educational point of view this is probably the easiest thing to impart. You give the coachee the book to read, the formulae to learn or you simply brief them verbally. Similarly, it is relatively easy to assess whether someone has the knowledge required; you ask or test them. The next level involves the development of skills. With skills, the process of development may take longer; this is about applying the knowledge. This could take place in the working environment or in an educational environment such as a workshop. If the skill level is about 'I can', then the next level is really about motivation or 'I will' . As management development practitioners, we often see people who have a good intellectual knowledge of a subject – that is, they 'know' and have the skills and even demonstrate these in a developmental session – but fail to incorporate such knowledge and skills into their working practices. This is often because the individual has no real motivation or intention of changing their behaviour. For the coach it can be immensely frustrating to see someone who clearly has the requisite abilities and skills but for some reason, often motivational, does not use them.

Consider, in this respect, the case study below.

CASE STUDY: DIFFICULTIES IN EFFECTING PERSONAL CHANGE

Andrew is a 42-year-old man who holds a senior managerial marketing role in an organization which is an international world leader in the manufacture of kitchen products. His educational background is impressive. He gained his first degree in Electrical Engineering and a Masters in Business Administration. In addition to this he has attended numerous internal and external training courses. However, he readily admits that most of these were of a technical nature.

He attended a management training programme, and his personal goals were to become more assertive, to feel more comfortable in confrontation situations and to learn to say 'No' without feeling guilty.

In many ways, Andrew was a model participant. He quickly became involved in all exercises, participated in all group discussions and his level of involvement and enthusiasm was high. The improvement in his performance was clearly discernible during the course of the programme. This was particularly noticeable in the sphere of assertion. Originally, he could have been described as timid, yet by the end of the programme he appeared comfortable in telling others what he thought, felt and needed.

Three years have now elapsed since Andrew attended the programme. During that time we have stayed in contact both by telephone and through informal meetings.

Our first meeting was over dinner about three months after completing the programme and we were amazed at the way in which Andrew's behaviour appeared to have regressed to the way it was at the start of the training. Indeed, during the course of the meeting we particularly observed that Andrew's conversation was self-deprecating and his style was apologetic. Furthermore, he behaved in a manner that was at the least passive and, at the worst, submissive. This was evidenced by the way in which he dealt with paying for the meal. The restaurant was one of the poorest we have experienced and the service was non-existent; indeed, Andrew himself, in his conversation with us, commented that this was totally unacceptable. When the bill arrived, however, Andrew enthusiastically proceeded to offer his credit card for payment and gave a healthy tip in cash for the waiters.

When we challenged him as to why his behavioural change had not been maintained, he was, as might have been expected, suitably apologetic. He provided the following explanation:

'Yes I know what I am supposed to do but somehow it just doesn't seem to work like that. It's not that easy; I felt uncomfortable. I found myself behaving in a way that wasn't really me. I felt false; the first time somebody challenged me I simply crumbled. It was easier to stay the way that I was.'

What he seemed to be saying was, 'I know what to do, I have the skills to do it, yet somehow my thought processes have not caught up. What is more, because in my head I still do not believe it, at the first sign of difficulty, it is easier to give up.'

Such is the challenge faced by anyone trying to bring about personal change. Furthermore, it is also a considerable challenge for the coach to face. As a coach how do you help the coachee who is facing all kinds of internal and external forces which are resisting change?

A key issue here is for the coach to help the individual understand the nature of the coachee's own self-concept and how this may be restricting development. In considering the development of self-concept we are really suggesting the need, when facing the difficulty of motivating others, to actually confront some of the cognitive or thought processes which may be inhibiting them. There are number of key concepts here. The first is that *meaningful change starts on the inside and works its way out*. Put simply, our actions are simply the result of our thinking and our feelings. We cannot expect to bring about change by focusing on the behaviour alone. We must also address the nature of our thinking. Consider how many people make a 'New Year resolution' in order to try to force themselves to change – and fail. The problem is that they focus mainly on the behaviour and, as with all 'white knuckle' change, hold on for dear life trying to make sure that they do not revert to the old behaviour. The fact is, however, that, for personal change to be sustained, the individual needs to think of themselves in the new way rather than force change by focusing on behaviour alone.

The next key concept is the influence of those people we refer to as 'experts'. These are the people we allow to influence our self-talk. Such supposed experts may not be experts in the true sense but are people whom we allow to infect our own thinking about ourselves. They may be, for instance, peers, parents, teachers, professors or managers. Such 'experts' may influence thinking positively but, more often than not, we have found it is the negative experts who influence an individual's thinking. Couple this with the power of 'self-talk' – that is, the way in which we critically evaluate our own performance, either positively or negatively – and we can see how a positive or negative 'self-concept' is developed.

When the coachee is facing a crisis of confidence or avoiding taking certain developmental actions, the critical role of the coach may be to encourage them to reflect on how their own thinking is influencing or restricting performance. The following types of question may be appropriate:

● 'How competent do you feel in this area?'
● 'How positive or negative is your self-talk?'
● 'Who are the "experts" who have, in the past or currently, influenced your thinking about yourself?'
● 'How much validity should you really place on their opinion?'
● 'How clearly are you really seeing things?'
● 'Why are you avoiding moving outside your "comfort-zone"?'

Often the role of the coach, in a motivational sense, is to encourage the person to push back their comfort zone and start doing things that may not feel too comfortable but are certainly developmental. There are three strategies which could be used here, and the appropriateness of the chosen approach will be partly a matter of judgement by the coach and may even be influenced by such issues as the personality and learning style of the coachee.

The first approach to mention is that of 'flooding'. This is where we throw the person in at the deep end and hope they will swim. Some do. Many do not. This is a high-risk approach and is one which we have seen many organizations take in, for example, the induction of their new managers. They will say on day one, 'Welcome to the company, here are your car keys, this is your office – best of luck'. Some people will rise to the challenge of this approach, whereas others will find it overwhelming. In the past this is the approach that was often taken in trying to help people overcome fears and phobias. They would be placed right in the middle of the sort of situation they hated and would either be cured or made worse. So flooding is a high-risk strategy but, where it does work, it can be highly effective.

By contrast desensitization describes the use of a more incremental, step-by-step approach in which the person is pushed outside their comfort zone much more gradually. It is slower, but safer, and is the approach taken by trainers in many training situations. So if a person has a fear of making presentations to larger groups of people, on the first day of a training course they would be faced with a low-risk challenge – say, introducing themselves to the group. Later they make a brief presentation to the group with time to prepare, and so on, until at the end of the programme they are making presentations to large groups for extended periods without preparation time, under the scrutiny of the videocameras.

Finally, there is another strategy that can be used to good effect – namely, the use of visualization or imagery as a way of helping counter the negative mental pictures which may exist in terms of self-image. Returning to the presentations example, the person concerned could take time out to mentally visualize the picture of success and the feeling or emotions associated with the desired outcomes. We are not suggesting here that simply thinking success will guarantee it, but for many years it has been recognized in the sporting world that mental practice can improve performance, and our own research in the corporate environment (Hale and Whitlam, 1995) supports this.

So a vital consideration for the coach, at this stage in the model, is how to engender in the coachee a good level of confidence which is likely to lead to a higher level of motivation.

Stage 5: Implementation

The final two stages in the model of coaching focus on implementation and review. Implementation here refers to the implementation of the development plans which have been previously formulated. Often implementation means delegating tasks and responsibilities to the coachee in order to provide new experiences and opportunities for learning. As far as delegating is concerned, the difficulty experienced by many managers is actually letting go of aspects of their own work which they feel possessive about. This may be due to a sense of insecurity in allowing others to take on new assignments and responsibilities or could be simply related to the fact that they feel only they can do the job to the right standard. There is no doubt that delegation entails an element of risk, but there is every reason to suggest that this risk can be managed. Furthermore, there may be a case for often venturing beyond the basic delegation of a new task or assignment in order to develop the coachee. Real growth comes from the process of empowering the coachee by passing over responsibility and decision-making discretion. Whilst empowerment is an overworked expression in the corporate world, and true empowerment might be more of an aspiration than a reality, there are two key considerations here.

At one level, empowerment concerns the skills of the empowering manager or coach and, at the other, there is the consideration of the behaviours expected of the empowered individual or coachee. Sometimes it is assumed that if we ensure that the manager shows the right empowering characteristic then success is guaranteed. Our own experience suggests otherwise. We have seen cases where, at a corporate level, much effort is put into formulation of an empowerment initiative with little consideration being given to how to engender the right behaviours on the part of the 'empowered' individuals.

First, let us look at the principles of empowerment. Empowerment is about passing more responsibility down through the organization, and one of the first issues to tackle must be to define, in as clear terms as possible, exactly how much decision-making authority or responsibility is being passed down. Included here might be reference to financial authority, responsibility for people or decision-making power. Sometimes it is difficult to be specific about this at the outset, in which case the skilful coach will communicate these messages by providing guidance and feedback in a more iterative way as different tasks are delegated. A good rule of thumb, though, is for the coach to give responsibility for the whole tasks or assignment to insist on completed tasks being received back from the coachee. Otherwise, there is a risk that the individual will tend to complete only part of the task with the expectation or experience that the manager or coach will take over responsibility for finishing off. An issue for judgement is to be able to match the level of work which is delegated to the requirements of the individual, and this means striking a balance between providing a suitable degree of stretch without overwhelming the coachee. Nevertheless, we are often amazed by the amount of wasted potential in organizations caused by a lack of willingness to delegate and empower those in more junior positions. Often this is due to a lack of awareness of the individual's current skill base in terms of, say, technical ability, language skills or qualifications, or is due to a tendency to stereotype someone as, say, the junior or the support person.

In order to back up the view that true empowerment is a two-way process in which success is determined by the characteristics of the empowering manager or coach and the empowered individual or coachee, we looked at the examples we could find of where it was being handled well and identified what we refer to as the seven characteristics of effective coaches and of effective coachees.

The seven characteristics of successful coaches

1   **They know when to suggest or require courses of actions and how to communicate with different individuals.**
    They recognize that on occasions, there will be a requirement to instruct in a

more directive way but on the whole they prefer to suggest and encourage rather than tell.

2   **They demonstrate in words and actions that they have trust and confidence in others.**
    They will allow others to take decisions and will support others even if, sometimes, the decision was the wrong one. They recognize that this encourages others to take risks and to move outside their comfort zone.

3   **They involve others in brainstorming and decision-making.**
    They encourage others to take part in contributing to decisions which are made. In so doing, they allow coachees to understand the challenge of decision-making and encourage involvement which, in turn, leads to a sense of ownership.

4   **They use mistakes as learning opportunities, and are tolerant of others' development needs.**
    Mistakes are reviewed constructively without seeking to find the culprit or apportion blame. They will be open about their own mistakes, as well as those of others.

5   **They provide regular feedback, emphasize the positive and never ignore poor performance.**
    Empowering coaches provide regular feedback not only through the formal organizational system or process, but also on a regular basis through informal discussion. They provide balanced feedback, identifying areas of strengths and areas for development or improvement.

6   **They reward or recognize those who perform above the standard.**
    They will motivate coachees by providing public recognition of success. Such recognition will be given when it is deserved, rather than overused and therefore devalued.

7   **They celebrate individual differences.**
    They recognize that differences lead to strengths in terms of teamworking and they will encourage different styles, skills mixes and personalities. This is in contrast to those who only recruit in their own image.

The seven characteristics of empowered individuals

As can be seen from the list below the characteristics of the empowered individual or coachee complement those of the effective coach, however they are worth listing because of the frequent failure to address these behaviours at the individual level.

1   **They take the initiative and do not wait to be told what to do.**
2   **They demonstrate a high level of personal responsibility for actions and consequences.**
3   **They effectively challenge decisions, policies or procedures, whilst always offering alternative constructive ideas.**
4   **They know when to seek help or advice.**
5   **They go beyond that which is expected.**

6   They show willingness to work with individuals who have different styles of operating.
7   They seize opportunities.

Stage 6: Review

The review stage is shown as the final part of the model, although it should be noted that the review should feed back into further identification of development needs so that coaching remains an ongoing process. The principal skill which the coach needs to demonstrate here is that of providing feedback, and all the principles of effective feedback discussed later in Chapter 5 apply here too. The only particular comment to make is that effective coaches do provide regular feedback and use it as a way of supporting performance on an ongoing basis, rather than seeing it as a special one-off event.

One technique which will help coachees reflect on their experience is the use of learning logs. This means simply asking the individual to reflect on what, as a result of their experience or learning, they wish to STOP, START or CONTINUE. In this way the person being coached is forced to reflect, and also encouraged to see in a balanced way, their strengths, weaknesses and development needs. The learning log should form the basis for a constructive review discussion with the coach.

The process of reviewing does not come naturally to all, although its importance should be stressed, especially in terms of processing learning. Mumford (1994) provides useful categorizations of styles with respect to how individuals approach reflection and review of their learning. He identifies four styles:

- **Intuitive** – where there is a preference for learning from experience but not in a conscious or deliberate way. Learning is assumed to go hand-in-hand with management.
- **Incidental** – where learning depends on chance and incidents occur that happen to prompt learning and review.
- **Retrospective** – managers preferring this approach will look back on experiences in order to draw lessons, particularly where prompted by mistakes or difficulties.
- **Prospective** – which includes components of the retrospective approach but incorporates planning in order to consider how future events could present learning opportunities.

In coaching others it is worth thinking through which style they tend to prefer and how to encourage them to learn through constructive reflection as well as how to anticipate learning opportunities from future events. It is this final point which leads us on to the subject of mentoring which is covered in some detail in Chapter 6. In that chapter, we will explore how, through a process of mentoring others, it is possible to provide career-related and psychosocial support which transcends the immediate job or role.

Competence	Description
Rapport-building	Initial and continuing impact by gaining attention, respect and demonstrating confidence. The ability to meet others and to be liked and trusted. Puts people at ease by building a close relationship of mutual respect and consideration.
Understanding	Able to actively demonstrate listening by verbal and non-verbal behaviour. The ability to pick out important information and identify underlying feeling. The use of a range of different types of open questioning, aimed at obtaining information. Particular use of behavioural questions which provide evidence of actual performance. Uses questions so as to be able to identify underlying attitudes, values and beliefs and recognize their impact on actual performance.
Delegation and empowerment	Able to delegate tasks, projects and assignments with clarity regarding responsibility, authority and support available.
Objecting setting	Able to set stretching, but realistic, objectives, communicate these effectively to the coachee and monitor progress against these targets.
Problem-solving	Able to use appropriate techniques with individuals in order to analyse problems, make decisions and plan action.
Focused feedback	Ability to provide focused feedback to others regarding their behaviour and performance which is specific and balanced.
Assertion	Ability to show understanding and to state what is thought, felt and to express the outcome that is desired. Includes ability to seek workable compromise or find 'win–win' solutions.
Self-development and practical learning	Demonstrates actions that show a level of continuing personal and self development, views learning in a positive light and as being available to all individuals. Recognizes that learning happens in all different types of situations and is not bound by constraints of formal training. Is broad in their approach in finding opportunities to learn. Uses reflection to consider how things might be improved.

Figure 4.8   Competencies of coaching

Summary

We have explored how adults learn and provided a detailed model of coaching that incorporates some practical tools and ideas for enhancing coaching within your organization.

As additional information, in Figure 4.8 we provide a competency framework for the coaching role. This framework has been developed from our own investigation into the behaviours of effective coaches, and has been used as a self–evaluation framework for coaches. Indeed, we have used this competency framework, combined with the stages of the model, to develop a coaching effectiveness questionnaire (see Appendix 3). This questionnaire has been used to assess the extent to which managers are operating as effective coaches and should be completed by the coach and at least three coachees to provide some structured analysis and feedback. Looking at the questionnaire, it can be seen that questions 1–12 cover the six stages of the coaching model, with two questions allocated to each stage. Questions 13–28 relate to the competencies of coaching, again with two questions for each competence. Results from the questionnaires can be consolidated and fed back to the coach in order help identify areas of strength and areas for improvement. If you are seeking to enhance your organization's approach to coaching then you might consider the use of this sort of questionnaire in order to identify, in a focused and non-threatening way, where managers need help in developing the skills of coaching.

In parts of the Allied Domecq business we have used this questionnaire to provide feedback to managers as coaches before the coaching training and some time afterwards. This has helped counter the difficulty sometimes seen from a management development perspective where managers will believe or state that they feel they 'do it already'. Because the feedback is focused around the skills and behaviours of coaching, and the coachees who complete the questionnaires are encouraged to use the full range of scoring, there will inevitably be some areas for improvement. Our preference has been to use the questionnaire in an open way – in other words, not anonymously. In this way, the manager receives feedback which they can use for improvement. If set up in a climate of trust and in the spirit of development, rather than pure assessment, the manager will usually be able to formulate an action plan to address real needs as seen by coachees.

At this stage of the book we again ask you to pause for thought and consider some of the concepts covered in this chapter with respect to your own experience.

PAUSE FOR THOUGHT

- *Consider the ways in which you like to learn best – would you describe yourself as predominantly an Activist, Reflector, Theorist or Pragmatist?*
- *Next consider the same question applied to someone you have to manage or coach.*
- *How do you think your respective styles influence your way of working together?*
- *What can you do to ensure your style of coaching matches with the needs of the person you coach?*
- *Consider someone whom you manage and, against the model of coaching, assess how effectively you feel you are coaching them. What are the areas where you need to provide more support and input?*
- *Can you think of situations where you have experienced the flooding approach to development? How effective was it for you?*
- *What about desensitization?*

- *What about visualization or the use of imagery?*
- *Which approach would you take in developing those people you coach?*
- *To what extent do you believe there is an effective coaching philosophy of leadership in your organization? What is your evidence for this?*

References

Hale, R. and Whitlam, P. (1995), *The Power of Personal Influence*, Maidenhead: McGraw-Hill.

Hale, R. and Whitlam, P. (1997), *Target Setting and Goal Achievement*, (2nd edn), London: Kogan Page.

Honey, P. and Mumford, A. (1992), *Manual of Learning Styles*, Maidenhead: Peter Honey.

Kolb, D. (1984), *Experiential Learning*, Englewood Cliffs, NJ: Prentice Hall.

Mumford, A. (1994), 'Four approaches to learning', *The Learning Organization*, 1(1), pp. 4–10.

Stata, R. (1989), 'Organizational learning: The key to management innovation', *Sloan Management Review*, Spring, pp. 63–74.

5

TARGET SETTING AND PERFORMANCE REVIEW

80 percent of American managers cannot answer with any measure of confidence these seemingly simple questions: What is my job? What in it really counts? How well am I doing?

W. Edwards Deming
Tomasko, *Downsizing*, Amacom, 1987

The objectives of this chapter are as follows:

- to discuss the subject of target setting and to consider the challenges of setting targets in different functions
- to demonstrate, with examples taken from real work situations, how to formulate targets
- to consider the importance of providing constructive and focused feedback in managing the performance of others
- to discuss the developments which have taken place in the area of performance review and appraisal
- to review the skills required and the key stages of the performance review interview
- to show the leading-edge approach taken by some organizations with what is variously referred to as upward appraisal, multi-rater or 360-degree feedback.

Managing performance through target setting

In many commercial organizations there has always been a keen emphasis placed on measurement. The sort of measures that have underpinned most activity and review of performance might be categorized as the 'hard' measures or outputs. In Chapter 1, we developed a model of behavioural-related inputs which we said contributed to task outputs or results. Target setting, as it is described in this chapter, focuses particularly on the challenges of formulating, with individuals, targets or objectives that are concerned with encouraging the appropriate behavioural inputs required for success.

In Chapter 4 we mentioned target setting as one of the steps in the coaching model; here, we discuss the subject in more depth since we consider the subject to be significant enough to justify its place as a key part of the overall model of performance management. Furthermore, we recognize that target setting often forms an integral part of an organization's in-company performance management or performance appraisal system.

We have argued throughout the book so far that, if we can define what success looks like in behavioural terms, we can use this behavioural profile to manage performance at various stages in the performance management cycle. All too often, managers are set 'hard' output-related targets, but are offered little or no guidance regarding how to achieve them. In more recent years it has been recognized that an overemphasis on hard targets can be self-defeating; managers achieving task-related results might, in the process, steamroller decisions, upset customers or suppliers, or indeed sacrifice quality. Such consequences clearly have cost implications but, as these costs are often hidden or disguised, such situations tend to persist.

First, a few comments on terminology. The words 'target', 'objective' and 'goal' are often used interchangeably and here we choose the word 'target'. As far as this publication is concerned, when we refer to targets we mean the formulation of a target which the individual agrees to work towards over a defined period of time and this is normally designed to help the person contribute to the organization's overall purpose. Additionally, many targets are designed to help the individual to develop. Ideally, members of the organization will work towards a number of targets that contribute to both the organization's and the individual's development; this fits with our view of performance management.

In terms of individual development, targets are normally set in order to provide a focus for the employee. They do not constitute the person's job *per se*. There will be roles and responsibilities, tasks and projects which have to be completed in addition to the targets.

So targets describe:

- conditions that will exist when the desired outcome has been accomplished
- a timeframe during which the outcome is to be completed
- resources that the organization is willing to commit to achieve the desired result.

'Standard' refers to an ongoing performance criterion that must be met time and time again. Standards are usually expressed quantitatively and refer to such things as:

- attendance
- manufacturing tolerances
- production rates

- quality standards
- safety standards.

Achievement of these standards does not necessarily move the job, individual or organization forward, but not meeting standards would have a detrimental effect. There have been some cases, though, of targets being set and rewards offered for achievements which should realistically be reached as part and parcel of the job. For instance, offering rewards for the achievement of certain levels of attendance would seem quite inappropriate, as full attendance should be seen as the norm in most contracts of employment. Rewarding attendance levels implies that full attendance is not really expected, whereas attendance is more an issue of standards than targets.

So how should you set targets? We have identified below a number of guidelines for developing targets drawn from research, our own experiences and organizational practice.

If you are in a senior human resource management role then you may well be aware of the requirements for effective target setting but, in our experience, very few organizations are as good as they could be in this area. Indeed, in reviewing with an organization the effectiveness and pitfalls of its performance appraisal process it is common to hear of difficulties in this area. As you read on, consider how well managers throughout your organization are able to set targets in this way.

1   **Include expected completion date or deadline.**
    Targets should incorporate some agreement regarding the completion date or when the target will be reviewed. When setting several targets, it is advisable to spread out the completion or review dates. With all the targets due to be achieved by the same date, there is more likelihood that the pressure to achieve results against targets will increase as the deadline nears. Of course, overall review might take place formally through the regular performance review process, but this should not prevent immediate review on completion of individual targets.

2   **Focus on a maximum of six issues.**
    If too many targets are developed, effort is likely to dissipate. Target setting is about focus, and this is an excellent example of where the Pareto principle or 80/20 rule should apply. Targets should focus on the 20 per cent of issues that will lead to 80 per cent of the results. It is preferable to achieve a balance in the targets that are set. Some will be organizationally-oriented, some departmentally-oriented and some primarily geared to meet individual development.

3   **Be achievable but stretching.**
    If targets are to be valued by the individual working towards them, they must be seen as realistic and achievable. However, the balance has to be struck between realism and providing a degree of stretch which will prove motivational. If the target is unrealistic, the individual will either fail psychologically to commit to working towards it or will strive to meet the target but will

be heading for a fall. Whilst there is a need to set a target which is seen as a challenge, for it to have a motivational effect it should be considered by the individual who is working towards it as something which could actually be achieved. In terms of motivation, the manager setting the target will need to try to create a picture of success – of how things could be: we know that nothing is ever achieved without the individual first having created a mental picture of success, and the manager's role here is to help create that picture.

4   **Be negotiated and agreed.**
Target setting, as with most aspects of performance management, should be implemented as a two-way process. The employee is committing to work towards the achievement of a target. However, a target setting system that states only what the person working towards the target will do is biased. The employee clearly does not work in a vacuum and is likely to be more motivated if there is an overt commitment from their manager stating what sort of help and support will be offered. Support could take many forms including:

– allocating budget
– providing coaching
– giving information
– facilitating relationships with key people
– delegating assignments.

Targets should be agreed by both parties, and much pain will be prevented by being as specific as possible at the outset by building in clear and common definitions of success. This will make the subsequent review of performance less controversial.

5   **Be subject to modification.**
The effort an individual makes in working towards a target takes place within a broader context, and it is unrealistic to expect that all other variables will be held stable over time. There will be changing circumstances that will impact on the ability to achieve or the speed of personal performance. This should not, however, be seen as a reason for accepting poor performance or excuses. Rather than waiting until the review of the target to discuss changing circumstances, these discussions should take place at the time. Such modifications should not be seen as the norm, and generally there is a need for people to take personal responsibility when considering the reasons for their level of performance.

A helpful mnemonic which needs to be embedded in the conscious of your organization and utilized when drawing up targets is SMART.

● Specific
● Measurable
● Achievable and accepted
● Realistic and relevant
● Time-bound.

EXAMPLES: MANAGEMENT TARGETS

Time management

Acquire and develop personal organization skills to improve productivity and performance. Should be able to plan personal and external time and resources to meet the requirements of the job.

Skills and knowledge to be developed by attending an off-job time management course and subsequent development of time management techniques and a personal planning diary system.

Success will be measured by ability to prioritize urgent and important work and a decrease in the number of crises occurring over the next six months.

Team development

Develop your team through the provision of formal and informal interventions so that the team understands its purpose and is able to operate without direct supervision, drawing on individual strengths. Team to successfully manage a major project to be completed within six months. Effective leader of the team to be appointed and accepted by team members and to manage team processes.

Recruitment

Recruit a deputy who will be able to manage the team and technical functions in your absence. Define the role clearly, attract a field of candidates and make the final decision. Review of success to be determined after four months, based on successful integration of this person and their ability to perform effectively against key performance indicators.

Examples of personal targets

It is not suggested that the process of setting targets is easy, and there are challenges that most people face because of the particular nature of a role or function. Here we provide some examples of targets, set in different areas, that can be used to illustrate and develop the target setting abilities of managers within your organization.

EXAMPLES: PERSONAL SKILLS TARGETS

Influencing skills

Develop effectiveness in influencing others where there is no line reporting relationship. Assertion without confrontation to be shown in encouraging suppliers to meet contractual obligations and internal support functions to work within internal service agreements. Support to be offered through attendance at an external influencing skills programmes. To be reviewed after five months.

Personal computing skills

Become familiar with, and competent in, the use of the internal Intranet and to be able to exploit the potential of the Internet in order to access relevant and timely information for the department. Additionally use e-mail package as the primary means of written communication with those in other locations. To be reviewed in three months by considering examples of work conducted using these media.

So far, then, we have provided some guidance on how targets might be formulated and some examples of a range of targets. Target setting is frequently built into an organization's performance management system and your organization may provide guidance on how target setting should be approached as part of a formal system. It is equally important as a process in the relationship between a manager and team members and, even if not part of the company's formal system, will help clarify early on what is expected and the particular areas to which individuals should be applying their energies. This will ultimately help when it comes to providing feedback or reviewing performance. All too often when managers review the performance of individuals the parties hold completely different views as to what was required. In other words, the manager and the individual have different mental pictures of what success looks like and, because neither has shared or expressed this to the other, this leads to wrong assumptions and misunderstanding. We have even witnessed the absurd situation where the manager is actually clarifying the target at the same time as reviewing it!

EXAMPLES: TARGETS FOR SPECIFIC FUNCTIONS

Finance

Work alongside other function heads to develop realistic departmental budgets that can be incorporated into the consolidated company budget to maintain effective spirit of partnership with departmental heads, whilst ensuring understanding of corporate policy and constraints. To be completed by end of financial planning period and assessed by seeking feedback from departmental heads.

Personnel

To develop a succession plan for the business by reviewing performance and potential of top 30 managers against future characteristics which should also be defined using an acceptable process of analysis. Succession plan to identify potential internal candidates for promotion to Director-level positions and potential gaps where external resourcing will be required. To be reviewed in four months through presentation of plan to the Managing Director.

Focused feedback as a mechanism for behavioural change

Having looked at the challenge of setting targets we now turn to the key skill of providing feedback effectively to others. If target setting is the front-end skill associated with the 'tell me what you want' aspect of performance management, then feedback is the skill integral to the 'let me know how I am doing' part of the process.

Arguably, one of the most important performance management skills is the ability to provide feedback to others effectively. Unfortunately, however, the very word 'feedback' has negative connotations. The need for organizational members to share developmental feedback is captured by the idea that 'we would all rather be damned by praise than saved by criticism'. Imagine your manager asking you to meet after work and when you ask what they want to discuss, they respond 'I just wanted to give you some feedback'. It would be quite understandable to feel your heart pounding as you worry about what you may have done or not done and what are you going to be reprimanded for. Indeed, in discussing this subject with a manager recently, we asked 'When did you last give some feedback to the people in your team?'. The reply was in itself revealing. He said, 'Feedback ... mmm ... oh you mean when did I last reprimand or discipline someone ... oh yes I did some of that last week.' This is one of the main barriers we face in trying to develop feedback skills and manage the process of providing feedback; feedback can be emotional and can have negative connotations. Clearly, many organizations need to take actions that make giving developmental feedback more of a cultural norm.

In order to explore the subject further let us consider the issue of feedback in the context of personal development. Figure 5.1 shows a model which is often

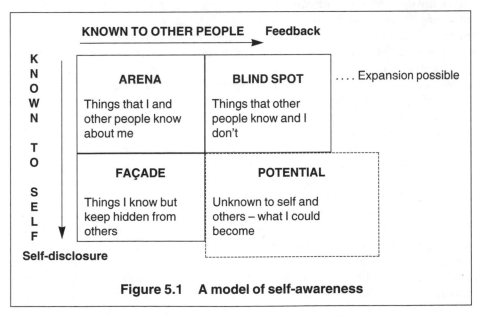

Figure 5.1   A model of self-awareness

referred to as the Johari Window. This suggests that, in our relationships with others, there are two dimensions to consider: first, what I know about myself and, second, what others know about me. Presented as a window with four panes, the model shows that there is an arena in which we interact with others where what I know about me is also known by others. When, for instance, we first meet another person and start to form a relationship, we put a limited number and range of items in the arena. This might include, for example, some factual information such as biographical data and some limited personal information of a 'safe' nature. In the top right pane is the section referred to as the 'blind spot'. This refers to information which is known to others about me but which I am unaware of. Included here might be mannerisms, habits and my impact on others. We all have blind spots, but, for some people, the blind spots are bigger – that is, in terms of the model, they have a larger blind spot pane. This is often the case for people who seem to be unaware of the impact of their behaviour on others. Next, the bottom left pane refers to things that I know about myself but which I keep hidden from others. This pane in the model is called the façade because it is behind this façade that the real person exists. Again, the size of this pane will vary between people. In the early stages of a relationship, the façade is normally larger as information of a more personal nature is withheld. It would be unusual, for instance, for someone to reveal information regarding their beliefs, values and faith at an initial meeting. Such information is revealed very selectively to certain people and only when the relationship has developed to a more advanced stage.

The model suggests that there is a fourth pane representing 'potential'. The proposition is that, in order to move towards the achievement of our potential, there is a need to decrease the size of the façade and, indeed, the blind spots. In other words, the façade can be reduced through a process of receiving and accepting feedback. Acting on feedback will allow us to modify behaviour in a way which is sensitive to the views of others. Similarly, by engaging in self-disclosure and revealing more of ourselves to others, we will create a climate of trust and increased openness. We have observed this latter point to be key to the development of a feedback culture both in organizations as a whole and in effective teams within organizations.

So, the model provides a sound framework for considering the way in which relationships develop and suggests that we need to be open to receiving feedback so that we might make behavioural changes which lead to personal development and organizational growth through learning.

Later in this chapter, we look at the mechanisms which are used to institutionalize the giving of feedback in organizations. The system may be referred to as performance appraisal, performance review or personal development planning – the actual name or title is not so important because, as we will see, it is how the system is implemented which really counts. However, with the growth of such formal appraisal systems, some managers have been naturally reluctant to provide focused feedback to their team members on an informal basis. Instead, they tend to 'store up' the feedback throughout the year in order to deliver it in full when the annual appraisal comes around. Such individuals view performance management from a narrow perspective. They restrict individual, team and organizational performance to the confines of the performance management or appraisal discussion. Managers with such a mindset, in our experience, fail to integrate learning and continuous enhancement of performance with the many rich opportunities for learning that exist within the workplace.

To help you and your organization develop a feedback culture extending beyond performance management systems we now explore the psychological responses stages which we often see people work through when they receive feedback from others. These key stages are shown in Figure 5.2. When presenting an individual with feedback which suggests the need to change behaviour or to develop new skills, the initial response is often 'denial'. If you recommend, for instance, that an individual could take a more participative, rather than autocratic, approach to management of people, at this stage the response is likely to be 'The only language people understand around here is that of the boss – you have to tell them what to do or nothing happens. Participation might work elsewhere but not here – we are different.' It is important to recognize that denial is a normal reaction to feedback and, at this stage, the best approach is not to respond emotionally but to simply present the evidence. In the example above, you might give evidence of how a participative style of management is used in other parts of the business, or of feedback from employees who expect a different style of management.

Next is the stage of antagonism, which is often linked to denial. This is where the receiver takes a more hostile approach and, in the example above, might take the form of such comments as 'Well all this stuff about participation is just a fad. I don't know why you can't see through it. Organizations are just talking about it because it sounds good – none of them really practise it.' The challenge for the person attempting to influence at this stage is to try to create a picture of how things could be, in order to move the other person through to the next stage towards acceptance which is 'mental try-out'. You will be able to detect that a

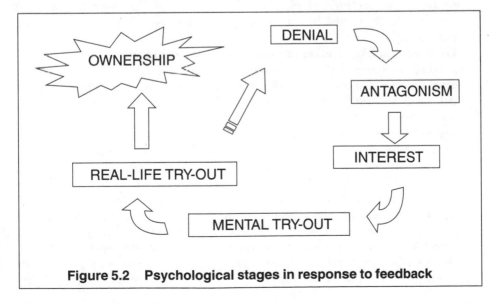

Figure 5.2   Psychological stages in response to feedback

person has moved on to this stage by the language used. They may say things like 'I cannot really see how it would work in my case', revealing that they are trying to visualize or see how things could be if they made the change which is being suggested. We know that mental try-out is always a precursor to 'real-life try-out' or experimentation. In encouraging someone to change, it may be possible to encourage real-life try-out by suggesting that the new approach or behaviour is used in small measures in a safe environment. If this is successful, then, ultimately, ownership or acceptance of the new behaviour might be expected. Equally, it should be expected that if the new behaviour – say, taking a democratic approach to managing people – fails, then this will serve to confirm the original rejection of the idea and the person will return to the denial stage of the model.

So what are the rules for providing effective feedback? As with the rules for target setting, we have identified a number of guidelines to follow in order to increase the chances of acceptance. These are the approaches and behaviours that need to be shown by those responsible for leading others, and you might consider to what extent these guidelines are actually followed in your organization.

1   **Focus feedback on the behaviour rather than the person.**
     It is important that we refer to what a person does, rather than comment on aspects of personality or character – in other words, we should describe behaviour in objective terms rather than make personal and, arguably, more subjective judgements. For example, we might say 'You were the highest contributor in the meeting in terms of the amount said' as opposed to saying 'You are a domineering person', so that we are not commenting on character traits but on specific observations. In commenting on personality traits we are really drawing our own conclusions and imposing these on the receiver but, by focusing the feedback on description, we are trying to remain neutral rather than engaging in evaluation. One approach is to couch the feedback in relative terms – by saying, for example, 'you were more vocal than other people in the meeting' or 'you used less direct eye contact when talking than the chair person did'.

2   **Give feedback soon after the event to which it relates.**
     Feedback is more likely to be understood and accepted if it is given shortly after the event. This enables the receiver to make the connection between behaviour and the feedback more easily. If it is provided at too late a stage, then a number of other activities will have taken place in the intervening period and this will tend to distort the receiver's perception. This, of course, is the difficulty encountered by many managers who use the organizational performance appraisal process as the primary vehicle for providing feedback. If the timing of the appraisal is predetermined by the system, then feedback may relate to events that took place several months beforehand. If the feedback had not been given at the time, then it will be less meaningful or, worse still, the receiver may not even recall the events being described by the provider.

3   **Provide suggestions for change in a tentative and supportive spirit.**
     We described earlier the stages that people proceed through on the journey towards the acceptance of change or feedback. It should be recognized that

personal change cannot be forced on another person, and the objective of the provider is to help the receiver accept the feedback and then decide to make appropriate changes in behaviour or approach. Change takes place from within the individual. Because of this, suggestions as to how the person could behave differently are best provided in a tentative spirit so as to allow the person concerned to work out for themselves how they would like to change. A number of possible alternatives might be presented or examples of how others behave could be provided. So, to continue with the previously used example, the advice might be 'You might consider how James operates in meetings. You will notice he uses a lot of open-ended questions and gets a high level of input from others before making decisions.... Sometimes I find it helps to just bite your tongue even though you may disagree with what you hear at the time ... often it simply gives another perspective and people feel they have a say in decision making.'

4   **Consider using the ABC technique.**
    A useful procedure to follow is to use what we describe as the ABC technique where:

    A = Action
    B = Behaviour
    C = Consequences

Here we start by describing the overall context of the person's actions (for instance 'You were taking part in a regular team meeting...'), lead to the specifics of their behaviour ('You tended to jump in at the start of the discussion of every discussion point...') and then describe the consequences of the behaviour ('It was noticeable how some members of the team said nothing to the meeting but engaged in side discussions'). As can be seen this final comment does not make a definitive statement of cause and effect, rather it is left for the receiver of the feedback to draw his or her own conclusions. The ABC technique is especially useful when the provider or receiver of the feedback could potentially become emotional, as it ensures that the behaviour is described and placed in context, devoid of emotive content. This is not to say that emotion has no place in performance management, and it would be unrealistic to suggest that emotions should be denied or ignored. On the contrary, for those providing and those receiving feedback there may well be a range of emotions to contend with. Techniques such as the ABC technique and the guidelines for providing feedback suggested here, though, do provide a way of distinguishing between the objective and the subjective.

Finally, on the subject of feedback, it can be useful to think of feedback as either 'developmental' or 'reinforcing'. The term 'developmental' can be applied to any feedback intended to help the receiver develop by changing their current way of operating. By contrast, reinforcing feedback is designed to reinforce existing behaviours and encourage the receiver to use such behaviours in a similar way in the future. Ideally, when presenting constructive feedback to others we should seek a balance, and one way of achieving this is to try to give one piece of reinforcing feedback to every piece of developmental feedback.

Having reviewed the principles for providing effective feedback, we now move on to consider the broader organizational systems which are used to aid the process of managing performance.

Performance review and appraisal systems

So far in this chapter we have explored two key skills or competencies associated with performance management, target setting and feedback. Arguably, these are skills that should be demonstrated by managers on a regular ongoing basis. However, in reality, these are key skills which often sit within an organizational performance review system. We now describe the evolution of such systems and provide examples of approaches that you could use to promote target setting and feedback within your team or organization.

As with many human resource systems, performance appraisal evolved out of a perceived requirement to institutionalize, and in many cases centralize, good human resource management practice. Personnel, or latterly human resource, specialists emerged and their role was one of ensuring both consistency of performance reviewing standards and a generally applicable measure of performance. Performance appraisal data often fed into other human resource systems such as those associated with training and development needs analysis, manpower planning and succession planning. Early appraisal schemes were set up in order to aid corporate decision-making, particularly for the purposes of salary review and promotion. In a simplistic sense, the assumption was that line managers concentrated on their line activities and the human resource manager was interested in the people aspects of management. This led, in many cases, to the 'disempowering' of the line manager and, in some cases, abdication of good people management practices to the personnel or human resource department.

More recently, however, it has been recognized that power should be handed back, often under the heading of 'empowerment', to line managers. This means that the role of the human resource manager in many organizations is geared towards facilitating, coordinating, identifying and spreading good practice. In some of the more forward-thinking organizations we are working with, performance appraisal systems exist primarily in order to encourage a healthy two-way discussion between managers and their team members regarding performance. In more traditional organizations, the system is seen as an end in itself; in such systems–driven organizations, managers are required to complete documentation because the rules say so. So the pendulum has swung back in the direction of decentralization, with the central function evolving into an empowering and facilitating role.

In tracking these overall trends there are a number of more specific developments which have taken place in the field of performance appraisal. It has been recognized that performance appraisal should be focused around competencies that are defined as relevant to the organization and the individual's job role.

Originally, assessment was carried out against commonly described generic traits on the assumption that there were certain traits that could be applied across the board for anyone being appraised. These might have included, for example, general headings such as 'communication skill', 'leadership' or 'commitment' – headings that were often ill-defined and applied to jobs where their relevance was questionable.

In the 1960s it was realized that a more systematic approach ought to be used and hence the management by objectives (MBO) movement gained in popularity. Here, the logic was that organizational objectives could be defined and then subsidiary objectives could be developed down through the organization. This was essentially a top-down process and, although very logical in design, MBO systems were often less successful in practice. Major criticisms of MBO were that it was implemented mechanistically and that objectives were imposed on subordinates from above. In addition, the style of assessment was clearly judgemental, and feedback would be given without the right to reply. In some systems, appraisal was actually conducted covertly, with employees being unaware of the assessment or grading accorded to them by their managers.

Early appraisal systems were applied mainly to managers as the term 'management by objectives' implies. Increasingly, however, with the recognition that the principles of objective setting and performance review can be applied to employees in most job roles, appraisal systems have been broadened in their application.

Many organizations now appreciate the value of making performance appraisal much more than a top-down only process. It is now commonly accepted that appraisal is more effective if appraisees have more involvement in the review of their own performance. Moreover, with the developments in upward appraisal, whereby the subordinate actually appraises the performance of the boss, performance appraisal has become even more democratized. This, in turn, has led to the growth in the development of appraisal schemes known as 360-degree feedback or multi-rater systems. Here, a number of perspectives are sought in evaluating an individual's performance on the basis that a range of people have an equally valid opinion or judgement to make. Later we show how organizations we have worked with are using such approaches as a means of providing balanced feedback to their people.

First, though, let us review some of the common difficulties experienced in designing a system of performance appraisal.

A common problem is deciding what to actually appraise. This presents a challenge for those designing performance appraisal schemes and often the difficulties lie in achieving a balance between providing certain generic criteria which can be applied to all employees and the need to recognize the individual nature of job roles. In many schemes we have seen in operation, the problem lies with ill-defined criteria for assessment. This invariably leads to participants feeling that they are being assessed against the wrong measures, and this in turn leads to a potentially destructive demotivated workforce. Ironically, considering that motivating people is often quoted as one of the aims of a performance management system, it is surprising how many organizations design and implement systems which do considerably more damage to morale than good. So getting the measures right is critical, and overall we favour the competency approach whereby critical behaviours for a job role are carefully and systematically defined and then built into the assessment process.

Having defined the key behaviours, it is necessary to build in an equitable scoring or rating system. In the past there has been much emphasis placed on using a numerical rating system, and it is now accepted by many organizations that numerical scoring can be extremely valuable so long as the system is simple to understand and it is clear how the score rating increments should actually be interpreted. Difficulties commonly arise where different scorers rate in a different way. So an individual in one section or department may be rated as '4' for their communication skills whilst in another section someone who actually performs better in this aspect of his job is assessed as a '3'. There are actually two issues here. First, there needs to be clarity as to how a '3' rating differs from a '4' and this must be clearly explained to assessors and those being appraised. Exactly the same applies to rating criteria expressed in word form, such as 'good', 'very good' and 'poor'; terms such as this rely heavily on the subjective interpretation of the assessor rather than making a commonly understood statement of assessment criteria. Second, there is a need for some kind of moderating activity to try to ensure that the hard assessors and the more lenient assessors align in terms of their approach. This role is typically taken on by a senior manager or the human resource function.

By contrast, some appraisal schemes rely entirely on what we describe as the 'free expression' or narrative approach in which the assessor completes the forms with written comment only. Although this approach has the advantage of allowing for supporting evidence to be referenced when completing an assessment, it has some disadvantages if relied on too heavily in that assessors will fill the white space to varying degrees – some taking the minimalist approach and others providing masses of data. On the whole, it is better to seek balance with provision for some tick-box style assessment and some narrative comment. Clearly, one should support the other.

Furthermore, it can, in our experience, be potentially damaging for assessment to culminate in one score or comment rating which is meant to summarize the individual's entire performance. In one organization we have seen a performance appraisal scheme in which the appraisee ends up with one of three overall comments 'below expectations', 'meets expectations' and 'exceeds expectations'. This proved to be extremely divisive for the following reasons: people tended to resent being 'summed up' in such definitive terms; they were unclear as to what each of these expressions actually meant; and they were extremely demotivated when they felt that they had at least maintained their level of performance but one boss had rated them as, say 'exceeding expectations' and another as just 'meeting expectations'.

Numerical or tick-box systems should also guard against the 'central tendency' which is where the assessor, when presented with an odd number of boxes to choose from, tends to choose the central or middle option. This tendency is reduced by presenting an even number of options, although even when this is done assessors will sometimes 'redesign' the form to include a central option.

Other difficulties experienced with performance appraisal include the use of the 'forced distribution' approach. This is where the assessor is forced to conform to an imposed quota which only allows for a certain number of people to receive ratings at specified levels. In reality it is unlikely that real performance will fit naturally with such distribution, and this leads to a classic case of the system driving the process or the 'tail wagging the dog'.

Of course, one of the biggest areas of debate regarding performance appraisal concerns its link with pay. It is now accepted that if there is a direct link between the appraisal interview and the salary review then seeking to achieve a developmental and open discussion with the appraisee regarding strengths and weaknesses can be difficult. If admitting to weaknesses could mean a smaller pay rise, an appraisee might consider it prudent to keep quiet at this stage. The difficulty occurs, however, when, as with most organizations, there is an intention of creating a meritocracy. If someone is performing well and this is agreed through performance appraisal, and successful performance is rewarded through the remuneration and reward system, then there is naturally a link. For this reason, a number of organizations now create some time distance between the appraisal and the pay review, whilst accepting that there is a connection between the two.

Forming at least some link between performance review and pay is likely to convey a message about the organization's expectations regarding performance and, in most cases, should help ensure that the efforts of staff are appropriately directed. Much of the research into pay and motivation suggests that money itself is in fact less of a motivator than we may have assumed in the past. Money motivates in so far as it allows us to meet our own needs whether they be needs for recognition, achievement or personal development. More important is the demotivational effect of an individual feeling that they are underrewarded compared to others in their work group or organization. This suggests a real need to ensure that the reward system, however closely linked to appraisal, is seen to be implemented in an equitable and defensible way.

Not all organizations work to a profit motive and therefore may not have the facility to reward individuals financially on the basis of performance, nor may they wish to do so. This may be the case in voluntary sector organizations, charities, some public sector organizations and organizations relying on voluntary, unpaid workers. If targets are set for teams and there is an element of team performance review, as discussed in the previous section, then it may be appropriate to reward team performance. Such rewards may take the form of a team bonus which is distributed amongst team members or could be incorporated with the individual pay review. Some organizations have found that, although team remuneration can help encourage team spirit and competition, it may restrict the extent to which teams will cooperate with other teams and can cause individuals to want to move to higher-performing (and therefore paying) teams.

As can be seen in this section, implementing performance appraisal is by no means a straightforward process. There are number of problems and pitfalls to consider from a design perspective, and we have touched on a few of the most common difficulties here. At this stage, however, we return to the perspective of the individual manager who has to conduct performance appraisal or review interviews with staff. Incidentally, we have used the content of the guidelines as an interview framework when researching individual and organizational competence in this area. This can be done by asking managers focused questions as part of a semi-structured interview. Such questions might include:

- 'How did you gather data on individual performance?'
- 'How did you brief the appraisee prior to the review meeting?'
- 'How did you plan for the interview?'

Compilation of data generated through such interviews can provide very interesting insights into the real behaviours and values attached to your organization's performance management system.

The skills of reviewing performance

Purpose, preparation and structure

Data should be gathered from as many reliable sources as possible in order to provide a balanced view on performance. Hard evidence should substantiate opinions. Spend at least as much time looking for strengths as weaknesses. Cover the whole period since the last interview, not just the last couple of months. Identify specific examples to reinforce feedback.

As performance in the current job is the main issue, gather relevant information concerning job requirements and establish job-specific and individual goals and standards.

Evaluate performance against expectations and note any variances which need to be discussed: beware of holding the appraisee responsible for factors beyond their control.

Sources of information might include:

- personal file
- previous appraisals
- other people the candidate works for
- a more senior manager/your manager
- the candidate's subordinates (with caution, and avoid hearsay)
- job description
- training plans
- disciplinary/absence records
- internal or external customers.

Prepare the paperwork thoroughly. This may include a review of the job description, targets and achievements and perhaps also some preliminary thoughts on completing the appraisal form.

Pre-briefing of the appraisees

At least a week in advance of the appraisal hold a pre-interview briefing so that the appraisee understands the format which you will be working to and has time to prepare. This will help you emphasize that it is a two-way process. Tell the appraisee when and where the interview will take place and demonstrate that it is important to you by honouring these arrangements and not rescheduling them. Explain the documentation which will be used: consider using a draft copy for preparation purposes.

Involve appraisees by inviting them to add to the agenda and allow them to feel that it is their interview.

Scheduling

It is good practice to schedule appraisal interviews so that they do not all take place during the same period; working from date of joining may be preferable and more practicable to interviewing all individuals in a fixed month.

The environment

Put aside adequate time for the interview, allowing time to write up afterwards; at least an hour should be allocated and you should be prepared to break and reconvene if necessary. The setting should be conducive to honest discussion rather than confrontation. Make sure that you will not be disturbed.

Drafting the interview plan

Consider what feedback you should give, identifying specific examples to illustrate comments. Anticipate the appraisee's reactions. Review relevant documentation and prepare draft points for discussion, remembering that your views may change following the interview. Decide on a structure with which you feel comfortable and which allows sufficient opportunity for the appraisee to present their own views. As with a selection interview, you need to strike a balance between having a structure, but not being so constrained by it that you are unable to be flexible during the interview.

Show your commitment to appraisal and development by stating the purposes of the interview in the form of a comprehensive agenda.

Arrange the appointment well in advance allowing time for the appraisee and yourself to prepare thoroughly. Allow adequate time (1–2 hours) for the interview and eliminate interruptions.

The structure depends on the aims of your appraisal scheme, but make sure you do keep to one. A typical structure for an appraisal interview designed to improve current job performance and plan personal development might be:

1   Review results against job description and agreed targets.
2   Discuss obstacles to improvement.

3   Set new targets.
4   Plan personal development.

During the appraisal interview

It is crucial to check that you are 'on the same wavelength' from the outset: restate your objectives and give the appraisee an idea of how you mean to structure the discussion. Your appraisal report form will often provide a useful, logical and meaningful structure to your discussion.

Seek the appraisee's views quite early on in the interview as to how well they consider they have carried out the tasks in hand and find out their reasons for this. This can provide invaluable help not only in establishing rapport between you, but also in your handling of essential feedback to the appraisee. It will help identify whether both of your assessments of performance coincide or where they differ. Remember, your initial assessment may need to be amended in the light of some crucial factors which you may have overlooked or had not been aware of beforehand. It also ensures that the employee has the opportunity to reap the benefits of any carefully prepared pre-interview self-assessment form. It is very important throughout the interview to convince the appraisee that you are interested in their points of view and that your assessment can only be completed in the light of what they say.

By gentle prompting and the use of open, rather than closed, questions, the employee can be led on to evaluation of their performance. Your assessment can be introduced into the conversation naturally and easily by way of commentary on what the appraisee has said. Indeed, managers often find that their employees are inclined to judge themselves and their performance more harshly than they would. Sometimes, however, the appraisee may gloss over negative points or skilfully steer the conversation away from them. It is up to you to bring them out and deal with them constructively, highlighting areas in which improvement may be required and how you will help the subordinate achieve it. Throughout the interview demonstrate a willingness to listen and to try to understand the employee's viewpoint. A very real problem in all interviews is that the interviewer can be so busy thinking of the next question that they ignore the answer to the last question!

You will want to emphasize good aspects of performance, both to reinforce them and to reduce defensiveness. If you can manage to discuss performance in a detached way, and focus on the job and actual examples of work, you will be more likely to have a constructive discussion.

It is your responsibility as a manager to give the developmental, as well as the reinforcing, feedback, once you have firmly established with the individual where this is warranted and identified the reasons for it. Inextricably connected with this is your responsibility to provide the means and wherewithal for improving performance. This could be by offering training, but could equally involve changing a work method or reassessing staff relationships. The important point is to clarify, within the interview, the action you and/or your employee will need to take and to record it. The opportunities for improved performance may well be reflected in new work objectives or specific tasks for the coming weeks or months.

Copious note-taking is usually unnecessary, can destroy rapport and definitely should be avoided, particularly when the appraisee is discussing sensitive issues. However, the noting down of key points is essential and does demonstrate your interest as well as providing a vital record of action agreed between you. It is useful to note your observations under the various headings of the appraisal form. Any necessary paperwork should be completed immediately after the interview while your memory is fresh. When scheduling an appraisal interview it is advisable to allow sufficient time for the writing up of the report, as well as for the interview itself.

End the interview when you consider that the goals for you both have been achieved. You may have to intervene firmly here if the stage of the interview has been reached where your employee has talked 'long enough' about future aspirations in the job or, indeed future career. Conclude by summarizing what it is that you have undertaken to do, together with the objectives for the next review period, and invite the appraisee to summarize the actions they have agreed, especially those which call for an improvement in effort on their part.

It is useful to agree on one or more review dates at which you can meet and check that the agreed actions have been taken. This review meeting should be scheduled and firmly written in diaries at the close of the interview.

Having looked at many of the common-sense guidelines for preparing for and conducting a performance appraisal interview, we will now spend some time considering the more leading-edge approaches taken by organizations that are innovating in this area.

Upward appraisal, 360-degree feedback and multi-rater systems

In recent years there have been a number of interesting developments in the way organizations approach appraisal and it is fair to say that some organizations are showing more imagination than simply taking the classic top-down approach, whereby the senior manager passes judgement on the subordinate.

In discussing this subject Mike Pedler, John Burgoyne and Tom Boydell (1991) comment:

> Appraisal systems usually don't work because they are done by 'bosses' to 'subordinates' and so are more about dishing out merit awards or apportioning blame than they ever are about development and learning from actions at work.

They argue for a mixture of self- and peer appraisal, with people working together both to identify performance measures and assess how they are doing.

The argument for peer appraisal is a strong one; it is well known, for instance, in the field of child psychology that a powerful way to influence children is through other children rather than relying solely on parental pressure. Similarly, there is much to be gained from encouraging peer appraisal in which one employee reviews and discusses performance with another on a similar level. Apart from the potential influence that such a review might have on the future performance and behaviour of the individual there are other advantages. Often a person operating at the same level has a clearer and more detailed picture of performance, whereas the more senior manager may be more distanced from the appraisee's job. Also, encouraging the exchange of considered and skilfully delivered feedback can considerably help improve communication.

There are, however, a number of potential difficulties with implementing peer appraisal. First there is a need to ensure that those appraising their peers are able to do so effectively, which means providing appropriate training and support – although, of course, the same obviously applies to appraisal delivered from the top down. There can be difficulties where there are personality clashes and when the peer appraisal affects the overall appraisal and the allocation of rewards.

Although there does tend to be a reliance on one-to-one appraisal there is much to be said for appraisal of groups or teams, and some would argue that the team is likely to be the primary performance unit in the future and that there should be a move towards the review of performance on a team basis, (see Katzenbach and Smith, 1993). Difficulties here lie in appraising the team, as a whole, when individuals may actually contribute at different levels and often some team members are more experienced than others.

There has also been a major growth in upward appraisal to the extent that some organizations have developed quite sophisticated approaches to the process of reviewing the performance of one's boss. In some cases, the upward review is carried out anonymously: the subordinate completes appraisal documentation regarding their manager and this will be sent to the personnel department who will process it, often integrating the results with the feedback from other subordinates. The personnel department will then prepare the feedback and deliver it to the line manager, sometimes also using the data produced from the upward appraisal process to identify training and development needs, potential problem areas or high potential staff for career development.

This anonymous approach will only work where the manager has a number of subordinates. The argument for making the upward appraisal process anonymous is that this is more likely to encourage an open, frank and honest appraisal of the senior person by the subordinate who could otherwise be intimidated by reviewing performance verbally. The disadvantage, however, is that this approach does not encourage a verbal discussion and, as the two people have to work together in the future, this is a wasted opportunity.

Some organizations take a partly downward and partly upward appraisal approach. However, where the upward appraisal process is added into an existing downward appraisal system, this often results in subordinates being reluctant to comment on their manager, or at least limiting themselves to generalized, positive comments for fear of recriminations at their own appraisal.

The following case study describes an initiative that represents a significant investment on the part of Xilinx, the US semiconductor organization. However, as we will show, this organization has taken seriously the issue of ensuring that the right measures are defined, using a competency approach that enables individual managers to receive focused feedback from a number of sources. This information then provides the basis for further development and training. Xilinx's 360-degree feedback process led to the identification of ongoing development needs, and specific training or coaching and mentoring initiatives were commenced.

CASE STUDY: USING 360-DEGREE FEEDBACK AGAINST DEFINED BEHAVIOURS (XILINX SEMICONDUCTORS)

Founded in 1984 and employing over 1200 people worldwide, Xilinx is a world leading supplier of programmable logic and related development system software. Programmable logic has gained acceptance from a wide variety of applications and can be found in products ranging from network interface cards to telephone switches, and from karaoke machines to ultrasound equipment.

Xilinx is a 'fabless' semiconductor company. In other words, it does not operate its own wafer fabrication facilities but concentrates on product design and market development. In the fast growing programmable logic market, Xilinx has found that a manufacturing strategy based on alliances is the optimal way of operating. The company is implementing a strategy of global expansion and considers Europe to be a crucial element of this expansion.

It is committed to developing a particular and well defined company culture, building on the strengths which its people possessed right from the outset. These are summarized in the company values statements which fall under the following headings:

- customer-focused
- respect
- excellence
- accountability
- teamwork
- integrity
- very open communication
- enjoying work.

Throughout 1997 and 1998 we worked with Xilinx on the implementation of a 360-degree feedback exercise for all the senior managers throughout Europe. Xilinx's approach had some distinctive features.

First, this was seen as an important opportunity to focus on the company values and, through a company-wide process, to ensure that they became much more than just praiseworthy words on a page or 'motherhood statements'. Not that this was ever likely to be the case: in contrast to the approach taken by some less progressive organizations, rather than simply defining the values at the top and announcing them to the employees, the first draft was developed and then worked through with every member of the organization in a series of workshops. This led to the publication of a revised version of the values which incorporated the views of people at all levels. For example, it was felt that emphasis should be placed on encouraging members of the organization to achieve a balance of interest in their lives, rather than being solely concerned with work.

The research regarding the definitions of successful performance was carried out with senior managers in Xilinx. The key behaviours were integrated with the Xilinx values and grouped into appropriate clusters, resulting in a 120-statement, forced-choice questionnaire with narrative comment sections for each cluster.

The senior managers were then assessed by their managers, all their peers in the management team, all their subordinates and, in some cases, by their internal customers. Confidential feedback discussions were held with each manager and, in conjunction with the independent consultants, personal development plans were drawn up. In addition, managers were encouraged to share a summary of the feedback with their own teams and to identify the personal goals and targets which they were committing to work towards in the future. Managers were setting up an informal agreement with their own people regarding how they intended to behave in the future and, for some, this meant entering into open dialogue regarding their own strengths and weaknesses. This is not something that has been common in the traditional managerial environment, but fitted absolutely with the concept of 'very open communication' as stated in the company values.

Overall, the process at Xilinx has meant that managers are assessed clearly against the preferred set of behaviours and that they cannot simply pay lip-service to the company values. This has also led to some revelations regarding managers who may have created a strong impression on one party in the process – say, their boss – but were not relating well to their own team. With direct quantitative comparison of perception by the categories of boss, subordinates and peers, such cases became obvious. Similarly, it was possible to see very clearly where managers had either an inflated self-perception compared to that of others or indeed where they had a low self-image compared to how they were perceived by others.

Summary

This chapter has provided a framework for target setting and examples of 'input' targets. We have explored the subject of feedback and appraisal reviews or meetings and given you a guidance framework for effective appraisal meetings before describing some of the more innovative approaches to reviewing performance. Next, we look at mentoring and its role in extending individual performance into the future. Before moving on, however, we again provide some questions designed to provoke comparison between those practices discussed in this chapter and those of your own organization, so once again ... pause for thought.

PAUSE FOR THOUGHT

- *How clear are the targets you and your team members work towards?*
- *Do these targets meet the SMART criteria?*
- *When did you last provide someone with feedback?*
- *How balanced was it? Did you provide evidence and examples to support the feedback? Was it both developmental and reinforcing?*

- *Can you recognize the psychological stages in the process of accepting feedback or the need to change in others? How can you help them through to ownership and ultimate acceptance?*
- *How effective are appraisal meetings within your organization?*
- *What are the strengths and weaknesses of the performance appraisal system in your organization?*
- *What can you do bring about improvement in either design or implementation?*
- *When did you last ask your own team or colleagues to provide you with feedback on your own performance?*
- *How open are you and your managers to the idea of asking for feedback on your own performances?*

References

Katzenbach, J.R. and Smith, D.K. (1993), *The Wisdom of Teams*, Boston, MA.: Harvard Business School Press.

Pedler, M., Burgoyne, J. and Boydell, T. (1991), *The Learning Company*, Maidenhead: McGraw-Hill.

6

MENTORING

An art can only be learned in the workshop of those who are winning their bread by it.

Samuel Butler, 1835–1902

The objectives of this chapter are as follows:

- to consider the place of mentoring in the performance management process and to review the likely benefits for the mentor and mentee
- to provide advice on how to set up mentoring in the organization, with examples taken from organizations we have worked with
- to look at the dynamics of the mentoring relationship and consider methods of matching mentor and mentee.
- to offer a checklist which you can use if you are considering setting up mentoring in your organization.

In Chapters 4 and 5 we explored the subjects of coaching and target setting and appraisal. In Chapter 4 we looked at how coaching can be used to develop the individual within their current role. The emphasis was placed on coaching as a process to support improvement and the implementation of learning in the job situation. Essentially, we argued that coaching is a process that is carried out by the immediate boss of the job-holder. In Chapter 5 we explained how the critical individual skills in managing performance were those of target setting and providing feedback, and we looked at how organizations are approaching the formal process of performance appraisal as a way of institutionalizing these skills.

We now move on to take a longer-term perspective in considering the individual's performance and examine how mentoring can be integrated into the performance management process. Mentoring as a theme has caught the imagination of those interested in the achievement of human potential in organizations in recent years, and we have worked with a number of organizations to support them in setting up mentoring initiatives. Despite our work and research in this area, however, there remain a number of key challenges to anyone wishing to set up an organizational mentoring scheme. There are a number of important considerations such as:

- Who becomes a mentor?
- Who is mentored?
- What is the actual purpose of the mentoring scheme?
- How do we match mentor and mentee?
- How do we manage the relationship between mentee, boss and mentor?

Understanding mentoring: definitions and benefits

Considering that the first references to mentoring can be traced back to Greek mythology (Mentor was the servant of Ulysses to whom the king entrusted the care of his son Telemachus) it might be surprising that there is no definitive formula for effectively performing the mentoring role. This is no doubt due to the fact that successful mentoring relationships rely in part on getting the dynamics right and, to an extent, this depends on something as intangible as human chemistry. Nevertheless, many organizations have set up mentoring schemes in recent years and it has come to take a more central role in the organization's performance management strategy, rather than being seen as an adjunct or an indulgence.

The increasing recognition of the part mentoring has to play in supporting the performance and development of individuals can probably be accounted for by looking at some of the more recent organizational trends.

As organizational structures become more blurred and ambiguous it is less easy to rely on one person – for example, the boss – for development. Increasingly, people report to several bosses, or their bosses change from one month to the next, or they do not actually have a boss in the traditional sense. Having a mentor as a constant point of reference provides a sense of security in an increasingly turbulent world.

The requirement for knowledge and skills is ever changing. No longer is it possible to rely on developing a skill-set through your early initial training and depend on this for the rest of your life. The need to develop new skills and acquire new knowledge increasingly means developing self-reliance and taking responsibility for your own development. A mentor can help by pointing you in the right direction and offering a broader vision.

As people progress in their career what is likely to distinguish them from others is not simply their level of knowledge and skill. They need to be able to navigate through the political minefield of the organization and beyond as well as understand how the organization works at a senior level. They need to develop a better understanding of how others think, feel and behave, since developing this sort of understanding is likely to lead to a more effective contribution. However, this kind of understanding cannot be taught through training courses and seminars; there is a need to be able to refer to the wisdom of a trusted senior-level adviser. And here the boss can only play a limited role because of the natural focus on the task, the interpersonal dynamics and vested interest.

Organizations have reported many benefits from setting up mentoring, including:

- improvement in morale
- reduction in labour turnover
- increasing motivation
- complements formal education and training
- better communication
- reinforcement of company values
- support of skills development
- identification of future leaders.

The emphasis of much of the work in the USA is on mentoring as associated with sponsorship and the concept of the protégé who is being groomed for future progression. In many of these cases the mentor is actually the boss. Our own preference, however, is to see mentoring in the context of performance management as giving an opportunity to support learning and the development of individuals. It is normally best conducted outside of the line reporting relationship, and mentoring discussions should be focused on the development of the individual which, in turn, leads to performance improvement.

From Richard Hale's doctoral research work in this field we would suggest that a mentor is:

> *an experienced individual, outside of the reporting relationship who, through regular meetings and discussion, takes a personal interest in guiding and supporting the development of a less experienced person in progressing beyond his or her immediate role.*

In our work with clients we have developed mentoring intervention strategies that are designed, above all, to enhance the learning of the individual. It has been recognized in such organizations that managers will often attend a prestigious business school programme, will feel positive about the experience, but nothing actually changes. It is here that an organized approach to mentoring, combined with an effective coaching strategy, can support performance improvement.

Although much of the work in the area of mentoring has focused on the benefits to the mentee, the benefits to the mentor in being part of a successful mentoring relationship should not be ignored. Those who have been part of a successful mentoring relationship in the role of mentor quote a number of personal benefits. One of the often mentioned motivating factors for mentors is that it helps fulfil certain basic needs to pass on one's experience and wisdom to others. This is referred to as a need for generativity and is characteristic of parent–child or grandparent–grandchild relationships. The suggestion here, then, is that similar needs are fulfilled through mentoring. However, benefits to the mentor may well be more tangible than this, as the following list suggests:

- The mentor sees things in a different way by using the mentee as a sounding board.
- Mentoring breaks down communication barriers associated with status.
- Mentoring provides a refreshing stimulus to renewing personal skills.
- Mentoring helps the development of problem-solving and communication ability.
- The mentor is seen by others as a developer of people.

Additionally, mention should be made of the equal opportunities issues associated with mentoring. Some have presented a strong equal opportunities argument for mentoring, whereas others have sought to provide evidence that many mentoring initiatives are, in fact, discriminatory. This would be hard to dispute, given that in most organizational schemes only selected individuals are offered the privilege of being mentored. The main issue is to ensure that the criteria used for selection do not unfairly discriminate against certain groups – say, ethnic or gender. Some organizations have, however, used mentoring as a way to provide special opportunities to certain minorities as a way of redressing the balance of power. Whatever the perspective taken, there is no doubt that being allocated a mentor through a formal organizational scheme gives the mentee opportunities not only to learn but to benefit from the senior-level connection in a career development and impressions management sense.

You may be wondering how to select your organization's cadre of mentors, and a significant consideration here is the critical skills and behaviour that are required by the effective mentor. In Appendix 4 we provide our own mentoring competency definitions using the behavioural profiling approach described throughout the book. You might wish to use this mentor behavioural profile in the following ways:

- to assess the effectiveness of current mentors in your organization
- to support the selection of mentors
- to underpin training and development in the skills of mentoring.

The behavioural profile shown is the ideal and we would acknowledge that, as with any behavioural profile, it would be unlikely to find a plethora of people matching this profile. However, you will need to make a judgement regarding those behaviours and traits which a person does possess and those which they may need to develop through the process of mentoring others.

Establishing a mentoring scheme

In establishing a formal mentoring programme for the organization there are a number of basic considerations. Those organizations which pay attention to these matters are more likely to find healthy relationships developing. Overall, though, the best the organization can hope to achieve is to create the environment for the relationship to evolve and to flourish; it is simply not possible to force the relationship to work. The first and most obvious, but often neglected, question is 'Why are we setting up mentoring?' Consider, for instance, whether it is about retention of key personnel, in which case this will help you decide who should be offered mentoring opportunities. Alternatively, is it about increasing management skills and knowledge for a select group – say, graduates or management trainees? Is it about improving the organization's visible display of top-level commitment to management development? If so, then it is likely top managers will be the mentors and middle managers the mentees.

Having decided who is being targeted for mentoring, the challenge to is find effective mentors and to manage the process of matching. Simply making an arbitary decision on how people should be matched is unlikely to be helpful and is probably analogous to setting up a blind date. You could be lucky and find it works, but the chances are it will not.

Consideration should be given to issues such as:

- Are the learning styles of the mentor and mentee compatible or complementary?
- Does the mentor have enough time to offer?
- Will the mentor be respected by the mentee? Does he or she have *gravitas*?
- Is there a match, or at least compatibility, professionally?

In the more successful mentoring interventions the training and development of the mentors is taken seriously. At Allied Domecq, for instance, potential mentors undergo a three-day mentoring and coaching development programme. They are introduced to the concept of mentoring, study the subject of adult learning and work through a major case study which raises not only the management and administrative issues associated with mentoring, but also ethical issues – for example, how to manage confidentiality and deal with conflict of interests. Participants also take part in a real mentoring discussion with one of their colleagues in order to better understand the process. They are then provided with a practical mentoring 'toolkit' comprising a number of exercises and diagnostic questionnaires which can be used in conjunction with mentoring meetings.

One of the other difficulties often encountered in setting up mentoring within an organization is the management of any possible conflicts of interest with the line manager. Just where does an issue cease to become something for the line manager to deal with and become an issue for the mentor to work with. Or should the individual seek counsel from both? And what if the advice is contradictory? What if the mentee has problems with their boss? Is it legitimate to discuss such matters with the mentor? What levels of confidentiality will be observed. In order to pre-empt a number of these issues, it is preferable to involve the line manager both in setting up the mentoring and in the training in order to understand the role and issues of demarcation. Some organizations advocate the use of a mentoring 'contract' which is drawn up at the start of the relationship in order to agree such issues as:

- amount of time to be spent meeting
- confidentiality boundaries
- mutual expectations
- relationship with the line manager
- review of the relationship clauses.

It is also worth raising the question 'Who mentors the mentor?'. In our experience it is important to provide support for the mentors, and it may be helpful to establish a key contact known as the mentor adviser who advises and provides guidance on the mentoring programme through implementation.

The case study below shows how mentoring and coaching have been implemented as part of a broader performance management strategy in a major international organization.

CASE STUDY: COACHING AND MENTORING AS THE KEY TO PERFORMANCE MANAGEMENT AT ALLIED DOMECQ

Allied Domecq Spirits and Wine is a truly international organization producing, marketing and selling in the drinks industry. They employ 11 000 people in 50 businesses worldwide and annually ship over 50 million cases as part of the £4.5 billion turnover of Allied Domecq plc. As part of their overall management development and performance management strategy, in 1998 they commenced the implementation of a global mentoring and coaching initiative. From a management development perspective there had been some disappointment at the failure of traditional business school education to deliver real results in terms of change and implementation of learning in the business setting. It was not that the education programmes were seen as weak, more that the level of transfer of learning could have been higher. The organization had previously developed a performance strategy that incorporated target setting, performance review and development planning. The systems associated with this strategy were reviewed at the same time as the launch of the coaching and mentoring initiative. A significant factor underpinning the performance management strategy was the competency framework. The company had identified a number of core competencies considered to be important for the role of a manager in Allied Domecq. In summary these were:

- clarity of purpose
- innovative change
- customer and market focus
- drive to achieve
- leadership and empowerment
- influencing
- confidence and integrity
- team commitment
- learning.

Definitions and behavioural indicators were identified at various levels.

A process for performance improvement built on three key factors:

1   performance management which aimed to optimize performance by means of continuous management support and feedback to individuals and teams
2   compensation management which aimed to optimize individual performance and motivation by differentiating compensation based on relative performance and achievements
3   employee development which aimed to help individuals plan and achieve their highest possible level of competence.

Successful performance for individuals was defined through the formulation of key result areas (KRAs) which are updated on a regular basis. These KRAs are mainly related to task outputs, although in recognition of the need to address the subject of behavioural competencies, or inputs, subsidiary objectives are defined around matters of business performance, people development and long-term contributions aimed at achieving sustainable change. Managers are encouraged to achieve a balance by incorporating behavioural objectives. On the coaching programme they are introduced to the Skills Analysis Questionnaire, as shown in Appendix 1, as a tool that can assist the identification of relevant behavioural skills.

There is a recognition that simply putting in place the system of performance management is insufficient. The company is implementing one of the biggest coaching and mentoring programmes in order to ensure that managers not only know of the relevant tools and techniques, but have the skills and motivation to develop their own people appropriately.

The coaching programme includes awareness training and skills development based on the model of coaching described in Chapter 4. This is being rolled out in areas as far afield as the Americas, Europe, Eastern Europe and Asia Pacific, with due consideration being given to issues of cultural sensitivity.

The mentoring programme entails a three-day course during which mentors are introduced to both the skills of coaching and mentoring. Workshops are intense with a high trainer-to-delegate ratio. Operational and ethical issues are discussed, and practice coaching and mentoring sessions are held.

As far as the mentoring initiative is concerned, the innovative part is that the senior managers are mentored by external mentors identified as being capable of adding value through the mentoring relationship.

It can be seen from the above case study how we are working with one major client to support the management of performance by addressing all the key stages of the performance management model described throughout the book. As far as the main emphasis of this chapter is concerned, however, it is interesting to note how mentoring is being used as a means of supporting senior managers in their long-term development. It was recognized that traditional executive education had limitations and, although mentoring is not seen as a replacement for such education, the idea is that mentors should help managers to exploit their work–based learning opportunities whilst keeping one eye on the future and their longer–term development. The use of external mentors to mentor the most senior managers was seen as particularly innovative and has proven a powerful developmental experience for both parties. The external mentor and the mentee gain insight into the other person's organization's sector and culture.

As previously mentioned, one of the principal challenges facing the mentor is to cope with the dynamics of the relationship from a management and an ethical perspective. Some of the potential problems here include:

● judging whether to get involved in discussing personal issues such as health and relationship problems
● what stance to take in conflicts between the mentee and the mentee's boss
● structuring the expectations of the mentee regarding progression and development opportunities
● clarifying what falls within the mentor's remit and what does not
● conflicts of interest between the mentee's behaviour or aspirations and the organization's values and the need of the mentor to maintain trust
● when to extend or curtail the mentoring relationship.

It was with these difficulties in mind that Richard Hale developed the case study shown in Appendix 5, which incorporates all of the above challenges and more, to be brought out through discussion in a mentoring skills training event. You may wish to use this case study or adapt it for use in your organization. It can be used to provoke discussion in an informal setting or used in more formal mentor appreciation training. A comprehensive version has been developed based on latest research and can be obtained from Richard Hale at rhale@cableinet.co.uk

The dynamics of the relationship and the challenge of matching

One of the principal challenges in setting up any mentoring scheme is that of achieving the benefits seen through informal mentoring where the chemistry works and the relationship just evolves. Although one might be expecting too much here, and could be accused of trying to 'engineer' what is essentially a human process, there are some interesting issues emerging from our work in this area.

We have looked in depth at over 100 individuals in mentoring relationships, drawing in particular on the mentoring schemes run by Scottish Hydro–Electric and Skipton Building Society where there have been conscious attempts to use mentoring as a means of supporting the performance management and personal development method. A summary of the findings is provided below.

Values are important when matching mentor and mentee

Organizations use a variety of criteria for matching mentor and mentee, yet there is surprisingly little research to suggest which approach works best. A key factor we have found is to do with the underlying values of the mentor and mentee. It would appear that these need to be compatible for the relationship to work. In one case, for instance, the mentee described how her mentor had wrongly assumed that she shared the same values as him regarding career aspirations and work ethic. In contrast with views of others, we found that biographic issues such as age and gender difference were actually less important in determining the viability of the relationship.

Similarities help speed up the relationship

A recurring theme was how mentors and mentees were able to build their relationship more speedily where they were able to identify between each other. This supports the well-known phenomenon of 'attraction to like' seen in much of the research in the field of social psychology. Similarities may have been to do with common interests, family background or similar communication style.

Contrasting personal styles can support learning

Many mentors and mentees suggested that the difference in terms of management or personal style actually helped in terms of learning. So those with a strong preference for action (Activists in terms of learning style) would learn from those who tend to reflect more (Reflectors). Those who were less confrontational would learn from those who engaged in constructive confrontation and those considered aggressive would learn from those who were more controlled. Those who were more operational would learn from those who were more strategic and so on.

Mentors often take part simply because it is an organization requirement

We found that many mentors were unable to state what their personal goals were when entering the mentoring relationship, yet several were able to identify certain spin-off benefits such as learning about another part of the organization, having to adapt their style to that of the mentee and being able to integrate this into their management style. It seems that more focused thinking about personal goals on the part of the mentor could lead to more learning opportunities being exploited. It is easy to fall into the trap of assuming that mentoring is mainly for the benefit of the mentee.

Mentoring supports the development of the less trainable skills and behaviours as well as insights

A key finding has been that mentoring supports the development of those skills and behaviours which are actually difficult to develop through traditional off-job training. For example, we identified evidence of behaviours such as team playing skills, patience, decisiveness and risk-taking being tackled. There was a great deal of evidence suggesting that mentoring actually improves the mentee's development by facilitating or providing insights. Insights are distinguishable from knowledge and skill acquisition, and we believe that the confidential and trusting relationship of mentoring allows disclosure, discussion and reflection which leads to such insights.

Where informal mentoring is already happening the formal relationship may not work

We found examples of mentoring taking place outside the formal company scheme. In these cases the individuals described having consciously built these relationships by finding or chancing upon a senior-level contact outside the line relationship. This was usually a person with whom the individual could identify and respect. Where this was happening it was interesting to note how the formally assigned relationships did not work so well. It was as though the organization's attempts to force a relationship were seen as less relevant, and overall this would suggest that maybe the human resources based scheme coordinator would have been better off enquiring where informal relationships already exist and offering support to these informal mentor/mentee pairings.

Some mentors will resist what they see as too much structure and intervention from the centre

We found that some mentors tended to resist too much intervention and direction from the centre – that is, from human resource or training and development departments. In these cases, the mentors suggested that the relationship should be allowed to evolve in as natural a way as possible and that there should not be too much emphasis on deliverable outputs as this would inhibit the relationship. This, of course, presents some challenges to those setting up mentoring and a need to strike a balance. There is a need to be helpful in providing resources, guidance and support to the mentors, but being too prescriptive can cause a backlash of resistance.

Richard Hale's research in this area continues but we can offer, at this stage, some practical guidance to those seeking to set up mentoring relationships. Below we provide a checklist which you can use to make sure that you have thought through the key factors.

Setting up mentoring: a checklist

1   Have you thought through the aims of the mentoring scheme?
2   Do you know where it fits in with other aspects of performance management – for example, coaching, training, target setting?
3   How should the target population of mentees be selected?
4   At what level should mentors be established?
5   Where is mentoring already taking place?
6   How can you support, or add value to, such informal unassigned mentors?

7   What sort of training should be offered to mentors?
8   How much structure are people likely to want in managing the relationship?
9   Who will advise and support the mentors?
10   How will you evaluate the success of the mentoring scheme?
11   How will you match mentor and mentee?
12   Will you do the matching or allow a level of choice and freedom?
13   What initial data do you need on the mentors and mentees?
14   What level of confidentiality should be agreed between mentor and mentee?
15   How would issues of ethical conflicts be managed, given the confidentiality of the relationship?

Summary

We believe that mentoring provides a great opportunity to enrich the development of managers and support them in their longer-term development. It should be accepted, though, that it may not be possible to create a 'road to Damascus' experience in all cases and there may be some strength behind the arguments regarding the difficulty in manufacturing or engineering human relationships. However, there is much to be learnt from looking at those cases where mentoring does work well and seeing how it is done. Having considered the issues raised in this chapter you might like to consider the following questions in respect of your own situation.

PAUSE FOR THOUGHT

- *Who has had a major influence on your own development, either in the past or currently, and, as such, might be considered as a mentor?*
- *Where in your organization are you aware of effective mentoring taking place informally?*
- *What can be learnt from this and could effective mentoring relationships be further developed elsewhere?*
- *How could mentoring fit in with other performance management and personal development activities?*

Further reading

Clutterbuck, D. and Magginson, D. (1997), *Mentoring in Action*, London: Kogan Page.

Hale, R. (2000), 'The Dynamics of mentoring as a route to personal and organizational learning', doctoral thesis, International Management Centres, Buckingham/Oxford Brookes University, UK.

Kram, K.E. (1985), *Mentoring at Work: Developmental Relationships in Organisational Life*, Glenview, IL, Scott, Foresman.

Mumford, A. (1993), *How Managers Can Develop Managers*, Aldershot: Gower.

7

INTO ACTION

There are risks and costs to action. But they are far less than the long range risks of comfortable inaction.

John F. Kennedy

The objectives of this chapter are as follows:

- to review the key points made throughout the book
- to provide a checklist to help you identify those aspects of the performance management cycle you need to address from now on
- to provide a format to help in formulating your strategy for influencing those in the organization whom you need to convince of the benefits of effective performance management, using the perspective specification approach.

A summary of the key issues

Throughout this book we have continually emphasized the importance of measurement. The key message has been that we need to become more scientific and objective in trying to define, measure and assess behaviours. In looking at some of the trends in performance management it was suggested that, whilst there has traditionally been a significant emphasis on managing performance by focusing on outputs or hard assessment of deliverables, there is an increasing recognition of the need to take a disciplined approach in dealing with inputs or behaviours. In fact, if the individual keeps working on the right behaviours, then eventually outputs will be achieved. Furthermore, if through a sound approach to defining the required behaviours in a job role, we can produce some sort of behavioural profile then this should inform the entire performance management cycle.

We proposed that a number of tools should be used in order to draw up the behavioural profile. We looked at a number of techniques that can be used in the context of investigative interviewing, such as the diary technique, critical incident and repertory grid. We are not saying that all of these should be used or that one is necessarily better than the other. What we are suggesting is that the more techniques used and the more people involved in the research in order to define role, the more valid the profile will be. In addition to the interpersonal approach of interviewing in order to define the profile we suggested a more mechanistic tool with the Skills Analysis Questionnaire.

Having defined the role in behavioural or input terms it is then possible to use this profile as the basis for selection. Those behaviours that are critical for success must either be present in those who are recruited or must be trainable. We believe that one of the most powerful approaches to identifying whether someone possesses the relevant skills and competencies is to use focused, or behavioural, interviewing. This is directed towards seeking evidence that the relevant behaviours have been shown in the past on the basis that this is a fairly reliable indicator that they will be shown in the future. In this way we can overcome many of the common difficulties of selection associated with distortions of perception. Getting the right fit between the individual and the job, as well as with the values of the organization, will help in terms of all the subsequent performance management challenges.

Much of a person's development and learning takes place in the real work environment rather than on management courses and education programmes. It is for this reason that we suggest that a critical aspect of performance management is to do with coaching in order to improve performance in the current role. Coaching means identifying development needs in a structured way and then considering a range of development options in order to meet those needs. In addition to this, however, the effective coach will help motivate the coachee and will challenge them to move outside their comfort zone. Coaching should not be seen as an additional management task. It might be seen as an overall approach or, as one company put it, aspiring to a 'coaching style of leadership'.

In managing performance we know that individuals need to be set challenging, stretching goals or targets and that these targets should address both the hard performance goals and the softer behavioural issues. By building this sort of target setting into the performance appraisal system and using it less formally outside the scheme, it is possible to stretch people beyond adequate to peak performance. Many people do feel they are exempt from such target setting for a whole host of reasons, mostly spurious. The challenge in terms of organizational and management development is to ensure that all parts of the organization are involved.

Finally in Chapter 6 we highlighted how individuals can be supported in their longer-term development through the formation of effective mentoring relationships. This is distinguished from coaching, which deals with the more immediate development needs, and supports learning which is not easily achieved through traditional off-job training courses.

Performance management: planning checklists

You are invited to use the checklist questions below in order to assess your organization's effectiveness in addressing those aspects of performance management discussed in this book. You can use this as a way of identifying specific action plans.

Approaches to measurement

	Agree	Not sure	Disagree
We put sufficient effort into defining behavioural inputs			
Different aspects of performance management are well integrated into a meaningful system (recruitment, coaching, appraisal, target setting, mentoring)			
There is a consistent approach throughout the organization			
Actions to take: Who to involve: Timescale:			

Defining success

	Agree	Not sure	Disagree
We use a range of interpersonal techniques and paper- or software-based tools for defining job roles			
We use a number of people in defining roles in order to see different perspectives			
We regularly review job role definition in order to reflect changing circumstances			
Actions to take: Who to involve: Timescale:			

Selection

	Agree	Not sure	Disagree
We use behavioural profiles as the basis for selection decision-making			
We use focused interviewing in order to identify behaviours in potential recruits			
We take a systematic approach to assessing whether potential recruits will fit into the organization in terms of their values			

Actions to take:

Who to involve:

Timescale:

Coaching

	Agree	Not sure	Disagree
We systematically identify the development needs of members of the organization			
We use a wide range of development methods other than just sending people on courses			
We actively encourage people to develop by moving outside their comfort zone			

Actions to take:

Who to involve:

Timescale:

Target setting and review

	Agree	Not sure	Disagree
We set people targets which address behaviours/ inputs as well as outputs			
Target setting is applied in all parts of the organization			
Performance is reviewed on a regular basis through joint discussion			

Actions to take:

Who to involve:

Timescale:

Mentoring

	Agree	Not sure	Disagree
We provide opportunities for individuals to form developmental relationships with senior people outside the line relationship			
We are aware of where informal mentoring is happening in the organization			
We know who would make a good mentor to others			

Actions to take:

Who to involve:

Timescale:

Formulating your action plan

Having read and interviewed the content of the book, and possibly having completed the diagnostic checklists and action plans above, you are now asked to further commit to action by considering those people who are likely to present the greatest challenge to your efforts. Specifically, what is it you intend to do, based on your current understanding of performance management? No doubt the challenges will entail influencing people at different levels and you will remember that, in Chapter 1, we suggested that the 'perspective specification' approach can help in planning to influence. We showed a basic perspective specification for influencing a senior director, a line manager and a team member. The format suggested was as shown in Figure 7.1.

We would advise that, having considered which aspects of the performance model you wish to tackle and with whom, and based on this assessment, you should draw up perspective specifications in order to help identify and ultimately overcome challenges.

Perspective specification *(State role or job)*	
Perspective	
(State likely perspective with regard to the aspect of performance management you wish to discuss)	
Possible objections/questions	**Possible responses**
(State here questions and objections you might anticipate)	*(State here the possible responses you could give)*

Figure 7.1   Perspective specification format

Summary

In this final chapter, we have summarized the main content of the book and have provided you with a structure to begin to plan improved performance management in your organization. We wish you success as you move into action.

Appendix 1

SKILLS ANALYSIS QUESTIONNAIRE

Purpose

The Skills Analysis Questionnaire is a tool that can be used to define success in a role by focusing primarily on behaviours. It can be used in its current form or can be adapted to the requirements of your organization.

Additionally, it can be used to help individuals reflect on their own strengths and development needs against the behaviours and skills covered.

Method for use

Issue the questionnaire to those who are helping in defining the behavioural profile for a job role and ask them to complete it following the instructions below. If using it to identify performance against the skills/behaviours listed then follow the relevant instructions below.

Collect and analyse the data from different sources. Discuss different perspectives where there are obvious differences and arrive at a consensus in terms of either the job behavioural profile or the assessment of individual performance.

Skills Analysis Questionnaire

Introduction

The following pages list a number of skills/behaviours/competencies which have been identified as possibly being important for successful performance in a range of managerial and supervisory roles in the organization.

The criteria are descriptions of behaviour and each behaviour is defined.

Obviously every job will have a unique set of criteria that relates to how success is achieved in that particular role. Consequently, there are no right or wrong answers, only an individual's perception of how successful performance might be demonstrated.

The questionnaire requires you to do two things, firstly identify the criteria or behaviours which result in successful performance of the specified role; secondly, to evaluate the performance of an individual against the profile.

Instructions for completion

(a) Read all these instructions before completing the questionnaire.

(b) Read all criterion definitions and descriptions individually and carefully. Do not make any judgements until this has been done.

(c) Rate the criterion according to its importance for success by placing one of the following numbers against the criteria:
   4. **Absolutely critical**   A person could not possibly perform satisfactorily in the job without a high degree of skill in this area.
   3. **Essential**   It would be very difficult for a person to perform effectively in the job without considerable skill in this area.
   2. **Desirable but not essential**   Skills in this area would sometimes enhance job performance, but satisfactory performance could be expected without this behaviour.
   1. **Unnecessary, not required or inappropriate**   Skills in this area would almost never have anything to do with achieving success in the job.
   0. **Detrimental**   Having this behaviour would actually be detrimental.

(d) Rate each criterion independently. Make your ratings based on your understanding of the job requirements.

(e) Please ensure that you use the full width of the rating scale available, you should aim to have no more than 12 behaviours rated as 4.

(f) Repeat the above steps, however, this time evaluate the named individual against the profile you have previously developed.

(g)   In completing this second stage you should rate against those behaviours you have shown as absolutely critical which you should list on the form at the end of the questionnaire.

(h)   In scoring this second stage of the exercise, the rating scales should be used as follows:
  4.   **Excellent performance**   Consistently performs above the standard required.
  3.   **Satisfactory performance**   Average.
  2.   **Below average performance**   But does, however, sometimes manage to achieve the standard.
  1.   **Poor or weak performance**

CORE COMPETENCIES

(1) LISTENING

Able to pick out important information in verbal communication. Paraphrases, summarizes and makes general emphatic reactions indicating 'active' listening.

(2) VERBAL COMMUNICATION

Displays effective expression in individual or group situations (includes awareness of non-verbal communication).

(3) PRESENTATION

Displays effective expression when presenting ideas or tasks to individual or to a group. Articulate and concise.

(4) INFLUENCING/PERSUASION

Able to gain support and respect for proposals across organizational boundaries and, where necessary, develop positive business relationships both inside and outside the organization.

(5) WRITTEN COMMUNICATION

Clearly expresses ideas in memos, letters and reports in writing, using the correct grammatical expression.

(6) TECHNICAL TRANSLATION

Converts information from professional or technical documents and other sources into an understandable format which is understood by a layperson.

(7) MOTIVATING OTHERS

Able to inspire and motivate others to achieve high levels of performance through words and actions.

(8) WORK STANDARDS

Sets high goals or standards of performance for self, subordinates, others and organization. Dissatisfied with average performance.

(9) PROFESSIONAL/TECHNICAL INTEREST

Actively studies information of a professional or technical area in order to stay abreast of/improve personal and professional performance. Builds 'expertise' in the eyes of others.

(10) COMMITMENT

Believes in own job or role and its value to the organization. Makes extra effort for the company, although may not always be in own self-interest.

(11) AMBITION

Has expressed desire to advance to higher job levels with active efforts towards self-development for advancement.

(12) SELF-DEVELOPMENT ORIENTATION

Takes actions to further improve skills and performance; makes active efforts towards self-development.

(13) ENERGY/STAMINA

Maintains a high activity level – for an extended period of time, when necessary.

(14) ATTENTION TO DETAIL

Completes tasks, has a thorough concern for all areas involved, no matter how small.

(15) CONFIDENCE AND INTEGRITY

Has the confidence to be honest and open in all dealings, and to respect and comply with core values and ethical principles.

(16) LEARNING

Able to constantly learn from experience, evolve capability and continuously improve performance to meet future business needs.

(17) RANGE OF INTERESTS

Has wide general knowledge and breadth of understanding of issues outside actual job, particularly events and/or ideas which impact on the organization or individuals who deal with their organization.

(18) INITIATIVE

Actively attempts to influence events to achieve goals; self-starting rather than passively accepting. Takes action to achieve goals beyond what is necessary; originates ideas and actions.

(19) DRIVE TO ACHIEVE

Able to initiate and deliver high-quality results consistently and to keep focused on improving performance, even in times of adversity.

(20)   TOLERANCE FOR STRESS

Demonstrates stable performance under pressure and/or opposition. This may be caused by time pressure, opposition of ideas, group pressures and/or task difficulty.

(21)   CONTROLLED DEMEANOUR

Skilled at maintaining composure and objectivity when confronted with personally defence-provoking or aggressive situations.

(22)   IMPACT

Creates a good first impression, gaining attention and respect, and demonstrating confidence.

(23)   RAPPORT-BUILDING

Makes an initial and continuing impact. Has the ability to meet people easily and be liked; to get along well with people and put them at ease; and to quickly build rapport through proactive development of close relationships.

(24)   INTERPERSONAL SENSITIVITY

Takes actions that indicate a consideration for the feelings and needs of others.

(25)   LEADERSHIP AND EMPOWERMENT

Inspires and motivates teams and individuals to achieve business objectives. Uses appropriate interpersonal styles and methods in guiding individuals (subordinates, peers, superiors) or a group towards the completion of a task.

(26)   FLEXIBILITY

Changes actions or behaviour in order to reach a goal.

(27)   NEGOTIATION

Communicates information or arguments in a manner that gains agreement or acceptance. Provides additional arguments or facts, in order to put their case to maximum advantage.

(28)   TENACITY

Stays with a position or plan of action until the desired objective is achieved or is no longer reasonable. Displays perseverance.

(29)   INDEPENDENCE

Takes actions in which the main influence is their own beliefs or principles rather than being influenced by others.

(30) TEAMWORK

Able to work cooperatively as a member of a diverse team and to be committed to the overall team objective, rather than the achievement of own interests.

(31) COMPLIANCE

Keeps to company policy and/or procedures. Seeks approval from the correct authority for making changes.

(32) ACCEPTABILITY

Personal style not likely to be abrasive or irritating to colleagues or customers/clients. Not likely to alienate others.

(33) ASSERTIVENESS

Able to confront others by saying what they want, think, need and feel but not at the expense of the other person. Seeks win–win. Able to say 'no' without causing offence or feeling guilty.

(34) RESILIENCE

Handles disappointment and/or rejection whilst maintaining effectiveness in role.

(35) CHANGE ORIENTATION

Willing to embrace and welcome change, rather than take a stance of active or passive resistance. Consistently seeks new ways of doing things.

(36) PROBLEM ANALYSIS

Identifies problems, finding relevant information, relating data from different sources and identifying possible causes of problems.

(37) VERBAL FACT-FINDING

Gathers information for decision-making through the effective use of questioning.

(38) INNOVATIVENESS

Creates and implements new commercial insights and the management of others. Generates and/or recognizes imaginative, creative solutions in work-related situations.

(39) DECISIVENESS

Ready to make decisions, render judgements, take action or commit oneself.

(40) ENVIRONMENTAL AWARENESS

Aware of changing political, economic, social and technological environment likely to affect the job or the organization.

(41) VISION

Able to stand apart from day-to-day activities and see the whole, focusing on major strategic goals rather than tackling each issue as soon as it arises.

(42) ORGANIZATIONAL DESIGN

Able to determine and develop the most effective organization to accomplish a task.

(43) PLANNING AND ORGANIZATION

Establishes a course of action for self and/or others to accomplish a specific goal; plans proper assignments of personnel and appropriate allocation of resources.

(44) SELF-ORGANIZATION

Able to efficiently schedule own time and activities.

(45) DELEGATION

Utilizes subordinates effectively. Allocates decision-making and other responsibilities to the appropriate subordinates.

(46) MANAGEMENT CONTROL

Establishes procedures to monitor and/or regulate processes, tasks, or activities of subordinates, and job activities and responsibilities. Takes action to monitor the results of delegated assignments or projects.

(47) DEVELOPMENT OF TEAM MEMBERS

Develops the skills and competencies of subordinates through training and development activities related to current and future jobs. This will include coaching as well as other on-job development techniques.

(48) CUSTOMER AND MARKET FOCUS

Able to understand the external world and the (internal and external) customer requirements as a part of developing long-term customer satisfaction.

(49) TECHNICAL LITERACY

Able to make use of information technology necessary to expedite work and/or as may be necessary to communicate fast and effectively.

(50) MONITORING

Oriented to attend to, and skilled in accurately evaluating, the performance and effectiveness of others and projects through observation and review of documented activities.

CRITICAL BEHAVIOURS (List here those skills rated as 4 or critical in the job)	PERFORMANCE RATING (1–4)

Appendix 2

EXAMPLES OF
FOCUSED QUESTIONS

Purpose

Here we provide examples of focused questions which were originally devised for one organization seeking to develop questions around its own corporate values.

Method for use

You might use these questions with discretion and judgement as they stand, if they are also relevant to your organization. Alternatively, you might use them to help in developing your own questions which are relevant to your own organization's values.

The questions

Customer-focused

- Who do you feel are the people you have to serve most in your current role?
  - How do you define their needs?
  - How do you measure your performance in meeting their needs?
  - How have you dealt with difficulties in meeting their needs? Give examples.
- How do you work with people outside of your immediate work area? Give examples.
  - Which people or departments do you find most difficult to work with?

- − How do you manage these difficulties?
- What do you see as the overall goals of your current organization?
  - − How do these translate down into your work area/job?
  - − What role have you had in defining the activities of your department/job?
- Describe a situation where you have experienced conflict between your job and the requirements of the organization/customer.
  - − What happened?
  - − How did things work out?
  - − What was your role?
- Give an example of where you have been able to contribute to improving or developing systems/processes/services in the past.
  - − What was your role?
  - − Who else was involved?
  - − What was their role?
- If this is difficult, describe how you feel things could be improved in your current role/organization. Give specific examples.
  - − What is the idea?
  - − How would it be introduced?
  - − What would your role be?

Respect

- Describe a major success you have had in the past.
  - − What was the background?
  - − What was your role?
  - − Who else was involved?
  - − What do you put the success down to?
  - − How did you celebrate?
  - − How did you recognize the contribution of others?
- Can you think of a situation where you have worked with someone who has a different style to yourself?
  - − Describe how you differed.
  - − How did you manage the difference in styles?
- Describe a situation where you have tackled another person over an issue or their behaviour.
  - − What was the background?
  - − What did you do or say?
  - − What do you feel was effective?
  - − What might you do differently if you were to encounter this situation again?
- How do you typically plan your day?
  - − How do you manage time?
  - − How have you managed when you have different demands on your time? Give examples.

Excellence

- Describe the methods and approach you have taken in facing a major challenge.
- What personal goals and targets have you set for yourself in the past?
  - How have you approached working to these goals?
  - What has been your progress?
  - How have you handled difficulties or setbacks.
- Think of a situation where you have been able to come up with new or different ways of doing things. What was the situation?
  - What was your role?
  - What challenges did you face?
  - Who were the people you had to persuade?
  - What approach did you take in persuading them?
- How do you keep up to date with your technical skills/knowledge?
  - How easy/difficult is this?
  - How do you track key changes in your field?
- What has been the situation in which you have worked the hardest?
  - What are some of the responsibilities you have taken on?
  - Why did you assume these responsibilities?
- How far have you gone in sacrificing your own personal comfort for the accomplishment of your team/role?
- How do you approach your own personal development?
  - In the last year, what have you done that you would consider particularly noteworthy to develop yourself?

Accountability

- Where have you had experience of leading or managing others?
  - What were the challenges/difficulties?
  - How did you manage these?
  - How did you assign tasks?
  - How did you let people know how they were doing?
- Can you think of a situation where you have had to confront others for not doing what you felt they were supposed to do?
  - What happened?
  - How did you manage the situation?
- Can you think of a task you were working on where things went wrong?
  - What was the problem?
  - Who was to blame?
  - How was the situation resolved?
- Give an example of where you have spoken out to present a view/give an opinion/make a decision, which has gone against popular opinion.
  - What was the situation?
  - How did you approach it?
  - How did you feel?
  - What happened in the end?

- When have you had to tell someone else they are not doing what you expect of them?
  - How did you approach the confrontation?
  - What was their reaction?
  - How do you feel you handled it?
  - What would you do differently?
- What is the established chain of command where you work currently?
  - In which situations have you stepped outside of it or challenged the leadership?
  - Why?
  - How was this received?
- What specifically do you do to set an example to others in your life/job?

Teamwork

- When have you had to go along with a group activity that is of no real personal interest?
  - How did you cope with this?
- When have you had to work with groups or teams where you are not a core member?
  - How has this worked out in practice?
- How have you contributed to team spirit?
  - How have you contributed to celebration of team success?
- What key behaviours/value do you feel you add to a team or group situation?
  - What is your evidence for this?
- Give an example of a situation where you have spoken out in a team situation, to challenge the views of the majority.
  - What did you say?
  - What happened?
- Can you think of a situation where you have had to show trust in other members of your team?
  - How did you do this?
  - Why was trust an issue?
- How have you encouraged contributions from new or quieter members of the team?

Integrity

- Give an example of where you have felt compelled to adjust the rules according to the circumstances or situation.
- What sort of standards (social, ethical and organizational) do you set?
  - When have these been challenged?
  - How did you manage the situation?
- Have you ever challenged someone else over his or her honesty? Describe the situation and what happened.
- Can you think of a situation where you have had to use a hard-sell approach in order to push a product or idea? How did you do it?

- Have you ever been in a situation where the organization or others have tried to push you to do something you have considered wrong in principle?
  - What happened?
  - What did you end up doing?
  - How did you cope with this internally/personally?
- Have you ever broken a company rule?
  - What was the rule?
  - Why did you break it?
  - What were the consequences?
- When have you had to tell a 'white lie'? Why? Give an example.
- Has there ever been a situation where you have had to do something other than you said you would do?

Very open communication

- Consider a situation where you have been criticized or given negative feedback. What was the criticism?
  - How valid do you feel it was?
  - How did you handle it?
- Give an example of a situation where you have had a difference of opinion with another person.
  - What was it about?
  - How did you handle it?
  - How was it resolved?
- Are you ever privy to information which you feel should be withheld from others? Give examples.
  - What determines who is given the information and who does not?
- Give an example of where you have given feedback of a personal nature to another person.
  - What was the background to the situation?
  - What was difficult about this?
  - How did you handle it?
  - Is there anything you would do differently?
- What do you consider to be your main strengths and weaknesses?
  - How do you exploit your strengths?
  - How do you try to overcome your weaknesses?

Enjoying work

- Describe your social life. What sort of activities are you involved in?
  - What do you particularly enjoy about these?
  - How do you balance the time demands of your work and social life?
- What have you done recently for the first time? How did you enjoy it?
- Can you think of a situation where you have celebrated a personal/family/ work success recently?

-    — What was your role in the celebration?
-    — Whom did you involve and why?
- ● What sort of priority does your work take in your life?
-    — To what extent do work and leisure mix in your life?
- ● What recent responsibilities have you taken on? Why?

Appendix 3

COACHING EFFECTIVENESS QUESTIONNAIRE

Purpose

This questionnaire can be used to provide a structured source of feedback on an individual manager/coach against the recognized competencies of coaching. It can be used as a one-off stand alone exercise or can be linked to a structured programme of coaching skills development.

Method for use

Ask those whom the manager has responsibility for coaching (either formally or informally) to complete the questionnaire and use the collected data to facilitate a discussion regarding coaching strengths and development needs. Use this as a way of helping individual managers see where specifically they need to improve their coaching skills and with whom, and to recognize their strengths.

Coaching Effectiveness Questionnaire

Introduction

The Coaching Effectiveness Questionnaire has been designed in order to enable managers who have responsibility for coaching others to received focused feedback regarding their coaching skills. This will be relevant for those with direct reports who they have to coach and those who have to achieve results through others. In other words, it is recognized that coaching often takes place outside of the line management relationship.

As the person completing the questionnaire it is assumed that you are coached by the person you are providing feedback to. It should be mentioned, though, that coaching can take place both formally and informally and it is seen here as a process rather than a one-off event. Essentially, it is about getting people to perform to the best of their ability in their current role by identifying and using opportunities at work as a vehicle for learning. The person receiving the feedback will be using it as a means of providing focus for action planning and improving the level of coaching provided to you. For this reason the questionnaire is **not** anonymous.

In completing the questionnaire please be totally frank and honest in your response. The emphasis here is more on providing quality feedback in the context of development, rather than assessment. We want those who have to coach others to know about both their strengths and areas for development.

Instructions for completion

1. Work through the tick-box sections ensuring you complete all questions. Please use the full range on the scale 1–4 using the following guidance:

    1 = Area of weakness
    2 = Some development needed
    3 = Meets expectations
    4 = Exceeds expectations

2. Where you have scored 1 or 4 please support your ratings with comments in the relevant comments section. Additionally any supporting comments are welcome. Feedback comments should be as specific as possible, giving examples from real experience.

Coaching Effectiveness Questionnaire

Individual ('Coach') Being Considered – Name:	Title:

Completed By (Coachee) –	Name:	Title:

Date:

1 = Area of weakness
2 = Some development needed
3 = Meets expectations
4 = Exceeds expectations

SCORE

1. Has a clear understanding of my role and how it relates to his/her role	
2. Has a clear understanding of the strengths and weaknesses which I have and which are relevant to his/her role	
3. Helps me to formulate clear goals and objectives in order to maximize my contribution	
4. Discusses with me, in a spirit of collaboration and support, those areas where I could improve	
5. Is aware of, and sensitive to, my own personality and style of operating	
6. Provides useful ideas about ways and means that I could draw on in order to develop my skills	
7. Motivates and inspires me through his/her enthusiastic approach	
8. Helps me to build positive beliefs about myself and about what I could do in the future	
9. Provides real help in assisting me to understand my strengths and weaknesses	
10. In dealing with me, always clarifies my scope and responsibility as distinct from his/her own	
11. Regularly reviews in a constructive way how things are progressing	
12. Takes time out with me for reflection and review	

COMMENTS ON QUESTIONS 1–12

Coaching Effectiveness Questionnaire

1 = Area of weakness
2 = Some development needed
3 = Meets expectations
4 = Exceeds expectations

SCORE

13.	Puts me at ease and makes me feel comfortable in his/her presence	
14.	Actively shows confidence in my abilities and potential as a person	
15.	Seeks to understand my perspective through the use of listening and questioning	
16.	Has an understanding of my knowledge, skills and attitudes relevant to success in my relationship with him/her	
17.	Works with me in order to define our respective roles and responsibilities	
18.	Offers and provides support to help me achieve tasks where I require it	
19.	Is clear and focused in defining goals and objectives for us both	
20.	Monitors progress against goals and discusses this with me	
21.	Shows how a range of approaches and techniques can be used in tackling problems	
22.	Uses both creative and analytical thinking in our discussions	
23.	Discusses how things are going and will give frank and honest feedback	
24.	Suggests alternative ways of doing things rather than having a single method approach	
25.	Approaches problems in a spirit of collaboration with a view to seeking a 'win–win' solution	
26.	Clearly states thoughts and feelings	
27.	Is a person who motivates me to continuously learn and develop	
28.	Demonstrates a personal commitment to his/her own continuous learning and improvement	

COMMENTS ON QUESTIONS 13–28

Appendix 4

COMPETENCIES OF MENTORING

Purpose

The competencies of mentoring have been drawn up to help organizations that are seeking to develop mentoring. The profile below of the successful mentor should be considered when seeking mentors, training them or evaluating their performance as mentors.

Method for use

Use the competencies of mentoring profile as a checklist to support your mentoring initiative. Adapt it, if you wish, to the needs of your organization.

ETHICAL

Commitment

Belief in the importance of the role of the mentor and its value to the overall business. Provides time and resources, although not necessarily in own direct interest.

Integrity and independence

Operates in a manner that is primarily in the interests of the mentee with particular regard to building and maintaining honesty, trust and confidentiality; does not allow self to be unduly influenced by organizational pressure.

INTERPERSONAL

Acceptability

Personal style is not likely to be abrasive or irritating to others. Does not place or use unnecessary pressure or demands on the mentee. Shows options and demonstrates choice for the mentee to decide appropriate course of action.

Rapport-building

Initial and continuing impact by gaining attention, respect and demonstrating confidence. The ability to meet others and to be liked and trusted. Puts people at ease by building a close relationship of mutual respect and consideration. Selective use of self-disclosure.

Listening

Able to actively demonstrate listening by verbal and non-verbal behaviour. The ability to pick out important information and identify underlying feelings of the mentee.

Questioning

The use of a range of different types of open questioning, aimed at obtaining information. Particular use of behavioural questions which provide evidence of actual performance. Uses questions so as to be able to identify underlying attitudes, values and beliefs and recognizes the impact on actual performance and potential. Uses questions as a way of enabling self-insight and learning.

Verbal communication

Maintains appropriate amount of verbal communication, does not use complex technical jargon, but prefers to speak simply, precisely and to the point. Uses tone and silences, as necessary, to prompt reflection. Supports verbal communication with appropriate non-verbal behaviour.

Sensitivity

Demonstrates recognition of what the other is feeling. Takes actions that show consideration of the needs of the other person.

Organizational sensitivity

Demonstrates the impact and consequences of specific actions on others and the business as a whole. Advises the other person to this effect.

COGNITIVE

Problem analysis

Can identify problems by logical analysis gained by the systematic collection of data primarily through accurate questioning. Can differentiate between cause and effect and suggests the need to address cause. Is non-judgemental, does not rush into suggesting actions but helps the mentee to resolve problems by suggesting process.

Creativity and innovation

Uses creativity to seek innovative or different ways of looking at issues, or for helping others find a more creative resolution to a particular problem. Challenges traditional ways.

LEADERSHIP

Leadership

Use of appropriate interpersonal style in guiding an individual towards a specific course of action or achievement of a task. Influences the other person and directs them to a goal without reliance on formal power or authority.

Empowerment

Takes whatever actions are required to enable the individual to achieve a particular course of action. Opens doors, provides access to people or resources. Helps facilitate. Does what is necessary to support the individual, without actually completing tasks.

ACTIVE LEARNING

Self-development

Takes actions that demonstrate a level of continuing personal and self-development; views learning in a positive light and as being available to all individuals.

Practical learning

Recognizes that learning takes place in all different types of situations and is not bound by constraints of formal training. Is broad in their approach in finding opportunities to learn. Uses reflection to consider how things might be improved.

Appendix 5

MENTORING CASE STUDIES

Purpose

These case studies seek to expose and raise for discussion the various administrative and ethical challenges that are likely to occur as a result of setting up a formal mentoring initiative. A more comprehensive version can be obtained or tailored for your needs – contact Richard Hale by e-mail at rhale@cableinet.co.uk or by telephone on +44(0)117 968 2299.

Method for use

There are two different scenarios, allowing you to work with two groups, as well as three episodes for each scenario, allowing you to build up a 'case history' over a period of time. This simulates the real dynamic nature of mentoring relationships.

Follow the instructions and issue the different scenarios at intervals allowing the groups to discuss what they would do in the circumstances. After each round of group work you should chair a discussion to identify the problems and possible courses of action.

Initial Briefing

Purpose

To explore key issues associated with the ethics and practical implementation of mentoring and the development of the mentor/high-potential employee relationship.

Timing

1.5 hours.

Instructions

In your groups you will be provided with three scenario descriptions which will be issued at different stages of the exercise.

You should read and discuss each scenario description when it is provided and then hold a group discussion in order to explore key issues and draw up an action plan according to the format shown below, which will form the basis of a final summary of learning points.

You should be prepared to present back to the facilitator and should present your action plan for each stage shown against the problems identified using the following format on a flipchart.

Problem	Action

At the end of the exercise you will be asked to prepare and present a group summary of the following:

- the issues and actions suggested
- principles that can be generally applied to mentoring.

Scenario description 1a

You are about to attend your first meeting with an identified high-potential employee in your role as mentor.

The background on this high-potential employee is as follows:

- very bright with high potential to become a senior team member in the future
- possibly overambitious in terms of time perspective and career aspirations
- high need for change and to be continually stimulated by new experiences
- forceful and confident style, directive and task-oriented
- works for a manager who may have plateaued – in many ways, has more vision for the future than his manager.

In the first meeting the employee reveals that he has told his peers in his team about the special mentoring relationship for which he has been specially selected. He says that some of his colleagues would like to set up such a relationship and has suggested that they might contact you directly. However, the others have not been selected as high-potential employees and you are wary about making a commitment. Equally, you do not want to dampen his enthusiasm. What do you do?

The high-potential employee's style in this meeting is quite outspoken, and he is openly critical of his manager. When you question him further it does seem that his boss's style leaves something to be desired. How do you handle this?

He states that he feels that his ability to really understand the business in his current role is limited and that he expects you to be able to help in this respect. What might you offer and how would you achieve this through his manager?

He also wants to improve his presentation skills but has already been through a basic presentations skills courses. What can you suggest?

Scenario description 1b

The high-potential employee has heard about the fact that, in the past, certain members of the company have been through a business school MBA programme and he believes undertaking this course is the only way to progress in the company. He quotes his predecessor who attended the programme and seemed to get a great deal from it. You, however, are aware that there are a range of other options regarding development and would like to explore these with him. You do not want to be seen as restricting his enthusiasm. What other options could you discuss? How would you persuade him regarding the value of these options?

The employee comes to the meeting having prepared a structured agenda for discussion and is clearly keen to make your mentoring relationship work. One of the issues he raises is basically very critical of his manager who has apparently been acting in what he considers to be an unethical way by taking gifts from business partners. When the high-potential employee asked his manager about this he was told 'You'll learn – this is the way the business really works. This is the sort of stuff they don't teach you on an MBA programme.' What is more, his manager is encouraging him to accept such gifts too. How do you handle this?

He goes on to reveal that he works with another team member who is very competitive, and there seems to be a fair degree of game-playing taking place, with this woman withholding information from him and failing to involve him in certain events and activities. Recently she tried to take the credit for a piece of work he had done. He has tried to confront her on this but she has denied doing anything of the sort. What can you, as the mentor, advise?

Scenario description 1c

In between the last meeting and the forthcoming one you have found out that the high-potential employee has quoted you as a senior source in a discussion with a member of human resources, saying that in principle you supported his sponsorship on an MBA. On a recent visit to the company this human resources executive raised the question with you in passing and had expressed some surprise. How do you respond to the human resources executive, the high-potential employee and anyone else for that matter?

The employee has been very diligent in following up on some of the ideas you floated with him at the last meeting, such as the need to arrange coaching in specific areas and attend a training course. He then reveals that the problems he originally faced with the difficult female colleague seem to have broadened to include other people. Some of his colleagues seem to resent that fact that he is getting special treatment as someone identified as having high potential and, consequently, have been excluding him from the information chain and failing to invite him to social functions. How do you, as a mentor, deal with this?

He has also received his performance review from his manager who, he feels, has been very unfair. He has been criticized on issues which he considers are to do with years' experience, rather than ability, and he feels that his manager is trying to restrict his development. He had refused to sign the appraisal documentation and is now seeking advice from you on what to do about it without being seen as a troublemaker. What can you do or suggest?

In addition, he has received a personal development 'report' produced by a consultant which he feels is somewhat damning. It refers to him having an abrasive style and he feels that it presents him as a 'maverick'. He has not shown the report to anyone else and is really angry with the consultant who, after all, is supposed to be helping him. The original idea was to use the report as the basis for discussion with his manager but he is reluctant to do so. What can you suggest?

He suggests that he should be transferred to another part of the business and wants to be placed with a more enlightened manager. What do you suggest or do?

Scenario description 2a

You are about to attend your first meeting with a high-potential employee in your role as mentor.

The background on this person is as follows:

● identified as a potential high flyer
● difficulties in terms of confidence, particularly relating to more senior people
● tends to underplay her strengths.

She seems very nervous in dealing with you, probably because she is intimidated by your seniority. Initially she will not really open up and is content to let you drive the discussion. How can you handle this?

Eventually she starts to open up and disclose more information about herself, and one of the issues you find out is that she has a history of mental illness. She tells you this in confidence and furthermore reveals that she has recently been suffering some recurrences of the problem which she thought was under control. What do you say or do about this?

She then says that she feels her lack of confidence may be related to these health problems, but there is no direct evidence. She maintains that she really does want help in overcoming the confidence problem because she realizes that it could be holding her back. What do you suggest?

She is clearly reluctant to be identified by others as a high-potential employee because she feels that this could cause some resentment and asks you not to reveal to anyone else that you have begun mentoring her. Is this a problem and what should you do or say?

Scenario description 2b

Prior to the second meeting you have been tipped off by a reliable source that the high-potential employee may have a conflict of interests with the company. Basically she has been seen mixing socially with someone who worked with a competitor and is now setting up a small business and poaching good people. How should you handle this?

At the second meeting the high-potential employee seems quite low and dispirited. After some exploratory questioning she reveals that she is experiencing difficulties in her personal relationship with her partner. They are considering breaking up. However, she is engaged to be married and the families have committed financially to the wedding. One of the big issues for her concerns her career. Her partner also has a powerful job with an international organization and has just been offered promotion. If she stays with him, her partner will almost certainly have to leave the country, as his posting will be abroad. She says that she is starting to question whether she should really continue pursuing a career at all. How do you handle this?

The other major issue that comes to light concerns her job. Her manager is pushing her very hard, giving her a great deal of responsibility and has just put her in charge of a major product launch. She does not really feel equipped to handle this, particularly given the level of financial responsibility. What can you do or suggest?

She has also been given much more responsibility for people and has to build a new team. She is concerned about her lack of people management expertise and where to start as far as recruiting and developing a team is concerned. What do you do or say?

Scenario description 2c

The high-potential employee reveals in this meeting that she has been offered another job which is on a part-time basis and involves working with a friend who has set up a small successful business in the programmable logic sector. She is not sure whether to accept. It would mean a rethink in terms of career and she is not sure about the entrepreneurial aspect. The advantages would be that she would be able to work from home. She has patched things up with her partner and they are planning to move about 100 miles away from her current office. What is your approach or response?

In addition, she puts on the table a report that has come into her hands from a 'contact' which has some really hot information regarding a competitor organization and suggests that you might be interested in taking a copy. She proposes that it could form the basis or a good 'mentoring' discussion regarding the changing shape of the industry. Clearly you would not, she says, be able to reveal the source of the information to anyone else. What do you do or say?

Furthermore, she has been attending an externally-run education programme which takes her away from work once a month. This has involved a significant time commitment but she is critical of the standard of the tutors delivering the programme and the organization of the whole programme. She admits that, on some days, she has not been attending and simply staying at home. This has allowed her to get on with some proper work in peace and quiet and she has actually been more productive than when at work. Of course, she has not told her manager about this. What do you do or say?

She asks that you continue to be a mentor for her if she leaves. She also wants you to give her a reference but wants you to promise that, if you are asked, you will not mention her difficult medical history and mental illness. What is your response?

Appendix 6

50 COMPETENCY DESCRIPTORS AND DEVELOPMENT IDEAS

Purpose

To provide a reference source for working with behavioural competencies. It is often considered difficult to define precisely what successful performance of a particular behaviour of competence looks like. We provide here some examples of how the behaviour might be seen and, equally, some of the negative indicators. In addition, we offer some thoughts on what can be done to develop each behaviour and have related this to learning style preferences (Activist, Reflector, Theorist and Pragmatist).

Method for use

You can offer this reference material to those who are concerned with either developing the competencies or behaviour described or those who are concerned with encouraging others to develop. You will see that the 50 competencies match those of the Skills Analysis Questionnaire in Appendix 1 and, as such, this material can be used in a focused way to pick out those behaviours or competencies that are identified as critical for success in the behavioural/job profile.

Introduction

We have taken each of the 50 competencies from the Skills Analysis Questionnaire and provided you with the following:

- **positive and negative descriptions of each of these competencies**
- **ideas for developing skills and understanding in each of these competencies**

This is done first to help you identify the individual's real development need and, second, to help you identify how you can provide learning opportunities for that individual.

Page layout

- **Description of the competency**
  Each section commences with a description of the competency.

- **Positive and negative indicators**
  This is followed by positive and negative indicators of performance.

- **Development thought-provokers – related to learning styles**
  This is followed by thought-provokers – suggested ideas for enhancing an individual's ability. Please note that the ideas are not absolutes, they are not the only way and they are not complete. They are designed to help you develop and identify how you can enhance someone's performance in the given competence area.

A thought-provoker is given for an Activist, Reflector, Theorist and Pragmatist for each of the competencies. The ideas given appeal to a particular learning style. For example, a Theorist is encouraged to read and develop conclusions. Clearly, you can work against or challenge the individual's preferred learning style by using a contradictory thought-provoker.

1   Listening

Able to pick out important information in verbal communication. Paraphrases, summarizes and makes general emphatic reactions indicating 'active' listening.

Positive Indicators	Negative Indicators
Uses open questions to explore the 'real' meaning in messages. Paraphrases the comments of others to check understanding. Keeps quiet, uses nods, smiles and prompts to encourage the speaker. Seeks to involve every individual in the group discussion.	Tends to do all the talking. Communications are vague and irrelevant. Misses important points; creates a subsequent sense of confusion.

Development Thought-provokers	
Activist	Force yourself to paraphrase the words of the speaker; ask the speaker to comment on the accuracy of your interpretation.
Reflector	Write down the key points from a discussion, present them to those involved in the discussion and ask for comments on the accuracy of your interpretation.
Theorist	Read *Impact and Influence* by R. Hale and P.J. Whitlam, published by Kogan Page, 1999.
Pragmatist	Try keeping quiet; try asking more open questions.

2   Verbal communication

Displays effective expression in individual or group situations (includes awareness of non-verbal communication).

Positive Indicators	Negative Indicators
Use relaxed authoritative tone of voice and positive body language.	Uses a single style, does not adjust to facial or body language cues from the listener(s).
Generates real interest from those listening – revealed through meaningful questioning and attentive body language.	Discussions lack structure often disjointed or repetitive. Fails to express own views in discussions.
Senses the individual or group climate; empathetic, adjusting content and style in order to relay the message.	Fails to share important information or ideas.

Development Thought-provokers	
Activist	Following a discussion, ask the listeners to provide feedback on how you could have improved the presentation of your ideas.
Reflector	Following a discussion, write down an account of what you said and how you think you said it; identify what aspects you think you could improve on.
Theorist	Read *The Handbook of Communication Skills* edited by O. Hargie, published by Routledge, 1996, particularly Chapters 1 and 2.
Pragmatist	Use the positive and negative pointers above to identify an area you could improve on. Develop a plan of when and how you are going to improve the aspect of your verbal communication.

3   Presentation

Displays effective expression when presenting ideas or tasks to individuals or to a group.

Positive Indicators	Negative Indicators
Introduces a framework for a presentation; an order that follows the 'This is what I am going to say, say it, this is what I have said,' principle. Involves all with eye contact and questioning. Brings ideas to life with examples, scenarios, fact and figures. Paints visual pictures in the listeners' minds.	Is unprepared; waffles. Displays disabling anxiety – mumbling and fumbling, for example. Uses a confrontational and alienating style – for example, pointing, aggressive posture, glaring. Is passive, timid and quiet in delivery does little to inspire confidence.

Development Thought-provokers	
Activist	Do a series of presentations; after each presentation ask people to comment on your presentation, not its content.
Reflector	Record (audio or video) your presentation; review it making notes of things you could improve on.
Theorist	Watch a video on presentation skills, *Speak to Yourself* from BBC Training Videos, for example.
Pragmatist	Watch other people presenting, list down what they did that worked or didn't work; use this list to plan what you are going to do differently.

4   Influencing/persuasion

Able to gain support and respect for proposals across organizational boundaries and, where necessary, develop positive business relationships both inside and outside the organization.

Positive Indicators	Negative Indicators
Creates a positive impression of self to others.	Creates a poor impression; low credibility as perceived by others.
Listens and questions in order to understand the perspectives of others.	Often expresses negative 'it's never going to work' defeated views.
Asserts own beliefs and ideas in discussions.	Fails to question, makes assumptions and offers ideas without establishing the views of others.
Demonstrates a degree of personal 'shifting' in discussion when required.	

Development Thought-provokers	
Activist	Identify a person you want to influence, identify how you will know you have influenced them and ask others who see your interactions to comment on how you could improve your influencing skills.
Reflector	Think about a time when you influenced someone. What did you do well? Why were you successful?
Theorist	Read *Impact and Influence*, by R. Hale and P.J. Whitlam, published by Kogan Page, 1999.
Pragmatist	Plan an influencing 'campaign' – who, when, where, how?

5   Written communication

Clearly expresses ideas in memos, letters and written reports, using the correct grammatical expression.

Positive Indicators	Negative Indicators
Creates documents that are simple in structure and easy to understand. Keeps volume to a minimum, placing only key facts in the main body of text and supporting information in accompanying documents. Uses language appropriate for the anticipated reader.	Documents are confusing in structure often without introductory information on layout. Language is full of jargon or oversimplistic. Documents contain spelling errors, changes in tense, poor punctuation and poor paragraph structure.

Development Thought-provokers	
Activist	Collect and then critique a number of published reports.
Reflector	Review a series of documents you have written.
Theorist	Search out and read books on report writing and correct grammatical presentation.
Pragmatist	Set yourself a target, such as no sentence to contain more than 15 words; apply the target to your document.

6   Technical translation

Converts information from professional or technical documents and other sources into an understandable format which is understood by a layperson.

Positive Indicators	Negative Indicators
Questions and listens in order to establish current levels of knowledge and understanding. Describes the context of this 'technical' information. Explains the 'technical' by creating analogies and metaphors, often painting visual pictures.	Uses the 'technical' without regard for listener's understanding. Belittles the understanding of the 'audience' when questions are asked. Expresses impatience at the audience's level of knowledge of the technical. Delights in distancing self from others through the overuse of professional jargon.

Development Thought-provokers	
Activist	Talk to colleagues about how they explain key concepts to laypeople.
Reflector	Recall situations where you have been describing something 'technical'. What did you do well and what can you improve?
Theorist	Read *The Handbook of Communication Skills*, edited by O. Hargie, published by Routledge, 1996, particularly Chapter 7.
Pragmatist	Identify what technicalities you might need to explain. Develop some metaphors that will help laypeople to understand them.

7   Motivating others

Able to inspire and motivate others to achieve high levels of performance through words and actions.

Positive Indicators	Negative Indicators
Tries to understand what values other individuals hold through sensitive questioning and active listening. Makes self available to others for 'non-task related' discussions – both in terms of time and disposition. Actively seeks to involve others, offering activities and developments beyond the routine.	Ignores differences, expecting everybody to be motivated by the same forces. Concentrates exclusively on the task, ignoring the interpersonal. Either consciously or unconsciously seeks to dominate activities. Either consciously or unconsciously fails to engage others in activities.

	Development Thought-provokers
Activist	Set different team members clear goals, review progress and ask each why they have progressed as far as they have and what is motivating them to complete the task.
Reflector	Observe a 'good motivator'. What are they doing well?
Theorist	Read *Organizational Psychology* by Edger Schein, published by Prentice-Hall, 1998.
Pragmatist	Identify a task you need to achieve, plan how you are going to achieve it, review how you are doing, explore 'with yourself' why you have, or have not, made progress – what is or isn't motivating you.

8   Work standards

Sets high goals or standards of performance for self, subordinates, others and the organization. Dissatisfied with average performance.

Positive Indicators	Negative Indicators
Has written and unwritten expectations of how individuals should behave and the quality of work that should be produced. 'Walks the talk' applying the same standards to own practice – sets standards through leading by example. Engages others in the development of standards, encouraging ownership of the quality of performance. Encourages others to identify how things could be continuously improved.	Creates a sense of 'so what?', 'It does not matter' and 'that will do' in the team. Fails to see own input in the delivery of poor goods and services. Will blame others for shortfalls and not take positive actions in order to change the situation. Demands one thing from team and then contradicts the demands with conflicting personal actions.

Development Thought-provokers	
Activist	Visit other organizations or departments to look at how standards are maintained.
Reflector	Review the existing documentation on work standards within your team.
Theorist	Read *Target Setting and Goal Achievement*, by R. Hale and P.J. Whitlam, published by Kogan Page, 1998.
Pragmatist	Conduct a survey asking team members to identify the standards that exist and the standards that should be introduced.

9   Professional/technical interest

Activity studies information of a professional or technical area in order to stay abreast of/improve personal and professional performance. Builds 'expertise' in the eyes of others.

Positive Indicators	Negative Indicators
Reads professional journals; shares the knowledge or ideas gained.	Rarely makes contact with individuals outside of immediate work vicinity.
Attends meetings of a professional association.	Unaware of the latest developments in profession.
Submits ideas and articles to a professional association.	Rarely communicates professional developments to others.
Involves self in research projects on areas of professional interest.	Does not try to influence the direction of the professional body.

Development Thought-provokers	
Activist	Meet with representatives of your association.
Reflector	Review back-copies of your association's journals; identify trends from the subject matter of articles.
Theorist	Read the last four copies of your association's journals.
Pragmatist	Diary in and attend your association's meetings.

10   Commitment

Believes in own job or role and its value to the organization. Makes extra effort for the company, although it may not always be in own self-interest.

Positive Indicators	Negative Indicators
Able to clearly articulate how their role sustains, enhances and improves organizational performance. Can be seen to push self towards ever-improving performance. Described by others as someone who is truly engaged in the organization. Is clear about own interests and values and tries to link and align these with the team/organization's activities.	Unclear about the team and organization's goals and how to achieve them. Uninterested in influencing the direction of team and organization. Unconcerned about the development or the growth of the team/organization. Not interested in own self-development. Complacent disposition; demonstrates behaviours that convey a 'so what?' attitude.

Development Thought-provokers	
Activist	Go out and talk to people about what drives them to make that extra effort.
Reflector	Think about aspects or tasks within your job on which you readily spend more time and effort. Why do these roles or aspects of your job appeal? What have you learnt about yourself?
Theorist	Discuss with colleagues how your role contributes to the success of the organization.
Pragmatist	Set yourself a target – what are you going to achieve by when – and then achieve it.

11   Ambition

Has expressed desire to advance to higher job levels with active efforts toward self-development for advancement.

Positive Indicators	Negative Indicators
Has a personal development plan that describes the component experiences that will support further career development. Actively looks for new work-based experiences that support career development. Engages in a wide range of activities, taking the time to reflect on these activities and learn from the experiences. Actively develops networks of contracts that can support career development.	Waits for opportunities to occur. Stays narrowly focused on the job, failing to make new contacts and seek new experience. Has little idea about longer-term aims and career goals. Rarely makes the effort to explore and enquire about the new.

Development Thought-provokers	
Activist	Seek out the experiences that develop the skills to help you achieve your personal development plan.
Reflector	Review your career. How far have you come? What roles gave you the greatest fulfilment? What do you want from work now?
Theorist	Read *Assessing Your Career: Time for Change*, by Ben Ball, published by the British Psychological Society, 1996.
Pragmatist	Write down what you want to be doing in one year's, three years' and five years' time.

12   Self-development orientation

Takes actions to further improve skills and performance; makes active efforts towards self-development.

Positive Indicators	Negative Indicators
Asks questions in order to understand. Has a productive mentoring/coaching relationship. Actively engages in development events; subsequently committed to experimenting with ideas gained. Takes new opportunities; takes time to reflect on experiences, develops new ideas and puts those ideas into action.	Keeps head down; concerned with just getting the job done using the same approaches. Closed mind to new methods. Unwilling to stop and consider own 'blind spots' and developmental needs. Has a limited network of 'like minded' individuals.

Development Thought-provokers	
Activist	Visit other organizations. Present details of your visits to team members identifying what you learnt during the visit.
Reflector	Spend time considering what has happened over a given period. Identify what you are going to stop, start and continue to do.
Theorist	Read about the different ways you can learn through work. Try Peter Honey's *101 Ways to Develop your People Without Really Trying*, published by Peter Honey Publications, 1994.
Pragmatist	Make public your commitment to use a different approach at work, for example.

13   Energy/stamina

Maintains a high activity level – for an extended period of time, when necessary.

Positive Indicators	Negative Indicators
Remains focused and enthused for the duration of the 'project'. Keeps going by knowing when to ease the pace and knowing when extra effort is required. Pulls people along with a positive disposition. Focuses on the key levers and the important actions in order to conserve energy level.	Does not know what needs to be done by when; consequently, goes 'into a spin' leading to exhaustion. Fails to take care of self, or to take time to re-establish energy levels. Continually creates a climate of demotivation by describing low energy and morale levels. Always identifies the problems and the causes without taking positive personal remedial actions.

Development Thought-provokers	
Activist	Set yourself small targets and reward yourself when you achieve them.
Reflector	Look back at how you maintained energy levels in the past; apply the lessons learnt.
Theorist	Read books on time management or stress.
Pragmatist	List the goals you want to achieve by when. Work on them.

14   Attention to detail

Completes tasks, has a thorough concern for all areas involved, no matter how small.

Positive Indicators	Negative Indicators
Has a clear picture of the quality of the final output. Communicates the expected standard to those around. Always references the current position against the future vision. Reminds others of when tasks need to be completed; breaks down the task into components for others.	Rarely sets personal goals. Rarely sets out detailed goals and expectations of others. Fails to review what has been achieved; always happy to move on. Makes errors in outputs. Falls behind deadlines. Output quality differs from the original vision.

Development Thought-provokers	
Activist	Lock yourself away from distractions and give yourself time to read everything slowly, at least three times.
Reflector	Identify occasions when your outputs met exacting standards. Why did this happen?
Theorist	Read books on improving your concentration skills.
Pragmatist	Set yourself very detailed targets describing what the final output will 'look like'.

15   Confidence and integrity

Has the confidence to be honest and open in all dealings, and to respect and comply with core values and ethical principles.

Positive Indicators	Negative Indicators
Expresses own beliefs and opinions. Acts consistently within own beliefs and ethical standards. Confronts others who flout organizational principles and ethics. Instills confidence and a strong sense of value in others. Takes stands and decisions for the greater good.	Evades, or puts off, tough decisions or discussions. Expresses one set of beliefs and then behaves differently. Is publicly disparaging of others. Fails to act on own judgement and take the initiative.

Development Thought-provokers	
Activist	Discuss with team members your hopes, aspirations and concerns.
Reflector	Think about someone you respected. Identify what they did in order to generate that respect.
Theorist	Read books on the subject of effective leadership.
Pragmatist	Periodically hold debrief sessions; describe mistakes you made and what you learnt; encourage others to be as honest.

16   Learning

Able to constantly learn from experience, evolve capability and continuously improve performance to meet future business needs.

Positive Indicators	Negative Indicators
Seeks genuine feedback from others.	Always covering up past mistakes.
Knows own strengths and weaknesses and is taking actions to enhance performance in these areas.	Makes no real effort to improve personal performance or the performance of others.
Is always enquiring.	Pays little attention to own experiences and experiences of others.
Takes new opportunities and risks.	Continually uses the same approaches to situations, holding an 'If it ain't broke then do not try and fix it' belief.
Shares and describes lessons learnt.	
Displays no defensive behaviour in relation to mistakes.	

Development Thought-provokers	
Activist	Ask for feedback.
Reflector	Keep a reflective diary – this is what I did; this is what I learnt.
Theorist	Write a paragraph that describes what learning means for you.
Pragmatist	Get yourself a mentor – someone who can support and guide you in your development.

17   Range of interests

Has wide general knowledge and breadth of understanding of issues outside actual job, particularly events and/or ideas which impact on the organization or individuals who deal with their organization.

Positive Indicators	Negative Indicators
Able to articulate a view of how developments, issues and events are interconnected and how those issues and events affect the industry in its local, regional, national and international context. Is able to see that many issues are more complicated and inter-related than initial first appearances. Actively seeks out and seeks to understand contradictory opinions.	Rarely stops to consider the consequences of developments outside the immediate working environment. Reluctant to step outside personal comfort zone to develop new perspectives of the industry in its local, regional, national and international context. Holds a simple polarized mindset which describes things as 'is' and 'isn't'.

Development Thought-provokers	
Activist	Join clubs; take on a public role – for example, school governor.
Reflector	Identify the legal, social, economic, technological trends, for example, that have influenced your organization over the last ten years.
Theorist	Pick three subject areas of interest and seek out published materials on these subjects.
Pragmatist	Enrol on a course that has nothing to do with your job but something to do with your organization's activities.

18   Initiative

Actively attempts to influence events to achieve goals; self-starting rather than passively accepting. Takes action to achieve goals beyond what is necessary; originates ideas and actions.

Positive Indicators	Negative Indicators
Holds a self–determining mindset – a 'life is what you make it' philosophy.	Demonstrates an unwillingness to lead and introduce adaptations.
Will take risks and experiment with ideas and new approaches.	Seems to wait for developments to have an impact rather than take action.
Displays a willingness to continually change and learn.	Reluctant to upset the status quo.
Doesn't wait for sanction; holds a productive air of impatience.	Holds a defeated and passive mindset – 'It's not going to happen and, if it does, then we can't do anything about it'.
Always suggesting new ways and approaches.	Demonstrates a dependency on the organization's leadership.

Development Thought-provokers	
Activist	Do something differently today.
Reflector	Think about the last time you changed something. How did you do it? How long did it take?
Theorist	Read R. Hale and P.J. Whitlam's *Practical Problem Solving and Decision Making*, published by Kogan Page, 1997.
Pragmatist	Identify what you are going to change and how you are going to change it.

19   Drive to achieve

Able to initiate and deliver high-quality results consistently and to keep focused on improving performance, even in times of adversity.

Positive Indicators	Negative Indicators
Able to articulate what needs to be achieved, by when and how.	Has no real vision of what needs to be achieved.
Takes actions to achieve goals.	Waits for events to help or hinder achievement of goals.
Continually seeks to improve the way things are done.	Does little to 'start the ball rolling'.
Exceeds expectations when delivering the results of projects.	Fails to deliver outcomes of acceptable standard.

Development Thought-provokers	
Activist	Present your vision to your team.
Reflector	Consider and identify the key issues you really need to focus your energy on.
Theorist	Read *Target Setting and Goal Achievement*, by R. Hale and P.J. Whitlam, published by Kogan Paul, 1998.
Pragmatist	Identify five things you want to improve about yourself.

20   Tolerance for stress

Demonstrates stable performance under pressure and/or opposition. This may be caused by time pressure, opposition of ideas, group pressures and/or task difficulty.

Positive Indicators	Negative Indicators
Keeps focused on the goals in the face of ambiguity, opposition and pressure. Able to deliver on a number of competing agendas. Remains controlled and clear-thinking as pressures increase. Is able to 'recharge' following pressure and learn from the situation. Recognizes when the pressure of work is impairing performance.	Loses a sense of proportion and works on the wrong things at the wrong time when faced with pressure. Concentrates on one thing at a time, excluding developments in other projects. Inclined to become passive or aggressive when the heat is turned up. Uses 'spaces' in work patterns to recharge and reflect.

Development Thought-provokers	
Activist	Create images or memories of less pressured times and call these to mind in difficult situations.
Reflector	Reflect on the issues that are really important to you.
Theorist	Read one of the many books on managing your own stress.
Pragmatist	Write clear task lists for the day and the week.

21   Controlled demeanour

Skilled at maintaining composure and objectivity when confronted with personally defence-provoking or aggressive situations.

Positive Indicators	Negative Indicators
Able to process the competing goals and pressures within a given situation and remain outwardly in control.	Responds to verbal provocation by either withdrawing, being manipulative or being hostile.
Talks down and defuses a situation when confronted with hostility.	Blames others for the situation.
Able to recognize the emotions being experienced and understand why those emotions are being felt.	Fails to understand what is being said. Misses hostile body language cues.
Strives to understand what and why individuals are saying what they are saying.	Uses inappropriate aggressive body language that further provokes the situation.

Development Thought-provokers	
Activist	Demonstrate that you are really listening and really want to understand next time you are faced with hostility.
Reflector	Think about the last time someone was hostile. How did you handle it? How could you have improved the way in which you handled it?
Theorist	Read G.M. Breakwell's *Coping with Aggressive Behaviour*, published by the British Psychological Society, 1995.
Pragmatist	The next time you anticipate a hostile reaction, think about how you could defuse that hostility.

22 Impact

Creates a good first impression, gaining attention and respect, and demonstrating confidence.

Positive Indicators	Negative Indicators
Uses appropriate greetings and clothes for given situations.	Fails to understand the listener's needs.
Builds credibility slowly.	Uses open and confident body language, coupled with strong intonation and clarity of voice.
Appears attentive and actively listens.	Appears distracted and uninterested.
Presents information concisely using appropriate third-party references.	Boasts of achievements.
	Gets names wrong.

Development Thought-provokers	
Activist	Ask people about their impression of you.
Reflector	Think about people who have created a poor impact and a good impact.
Theorist	List the things that lead to a poor impression. What do you need to do more of and less of?
Pragmatist	Plan how you can enhance the impact you create.

23   Rapport-building

Makes an initial and continuing impact. Has the ability to meet people easily and be liked; to get along well with people and put them at ease; and to quickly build rapport through the proactive development of close relationships.

Positive Indicators	Negative Indicators
Uses small talk – neutral subjects – to engage people.	Highlights individual differences.
Explores subjects and areas of common interest without being judgemental.	Freely offers opinions and prejudices.
	Talks about self.
Discloses 'personal' information – family, sporting interests and so on.	Discloses personal details early on.
Emphasizes similarities – 'Yes, I think that too'.	Fails to reciprocate when people disclose.

Development Thought-provokers	
Activist	Take time to engage in small talk.
Reflector	Think about someone with whom you have a good rapport. What do you do to maintain that rapport?
Theorist	Read *Impact and Influence*, by R. Hale and P.J. Whitlam, published by Kogan Page, 1999.
Pragmatist	Identify steps you want to take in order to develop rapport, apply some of those steps.

24   Interpersonal sensitivity

Takes actions that indicate a consideration for the feelings and needs of others.

Positive Indicators	Negative Indicators
Able to place self in 'other people's shoes'. Listens and then summarizes the feelings of others, using phrases like 'that must have left you feeling ...'. Mentally prepares for emotionally charged situations, trying to empathize with the feelings of others. Able to read the communication cues that give insight into people's real feelings.	Uncaring and dismissive of the feelings of others – a very matter-of-fact approach. Assumes how others are feeling and tells people what they are feeling. Does not anticipate the effect of actions or comments on individual emotion. Clumsy in conversation – provoking without thinking. Unaware of own feelings.

Development Thought-provokers	
Activist	Express how you feel in a situation; ask others to do the same.
Reflector	Write down how you think someone felt during a conversation with you.
Theorist	Read Daniel Goleman's *Emotional Intelligence*, published by Bloomsbury, 1996.
Pragmatist	Anticipate how someone will feel during a meeting. Think about how you will react.

25   Leadership and empowerment

Inspires and motivates teams and individuals to achieve business objectives. Uses appropriate interpersonal styles and methods in guiding individuals (subordinates, peers, superiors) or a group towards the completion of a task.

Positive Indicators	Negative Indicators
Lets people know what needs to be done, by when, and lets them get on with it. Provides support but does not provide solutions. Gives people the space to make mistakes and helps people explore those mistakes. Encourages people to reflect on the learning that has taken place, regardless of the outcome. Promotes the initiative and activities of team members around the organization.	Controlling; tells people what is needed and how it should be done. Fails to provide the individual with interim targets; chases the individual for progress reports at unagreed intervals. Is unavailable and/or abdicates responsibility. Encourages dependency by not encouraging people to learn from situations.

Development Thought-provokers	
Activist	Talk to team members about their expectations of a team leader.
Reflector	Think about individuals who are effective leaders.
Theorist	Read autobiographies of famous leaders.
Pragmatist	Identify five actions you are going to take in order to be a better leader.

26   Flexibility

Changes actions or behaviour in order to reach a goal.

Positive Indicators	Negative Indicators
Scans the environment, reads signals and listens to cues in order to identify when to modify plans and approaches. Questions and seeks feedback from all stakeholders in a situation; continually looks to modify and adjust in response to legitimate ideas. Actively seeks own different ways of doing. Communicates messages that indicate the direction of travel but not the finite detail.	Displays rigid and firm adherence to the goal. Has blinkered vision. Reluctant to listen. Has defensive reactions to expressed views. Fails to question and obtain feedback.

Development Thought-provokers	
Activist	In relation to a current goal, visit all stakeholders and seek their views on how the goal can be achieved.
Reflector	Think about your flexibility in relation to previous goals. How could you have improved your flexibility?
Theorist	Read *Target Setting and Goal Achievement*, by R. Hale and P.J. Whitlam, published by Kogan Page, 1998.
Pragmatist	Think about a current goal. Identify three alternative ways of achieving that goal.

27   Negotiation

Communicates information or arguments in a manner that gains agreement or acceptance. Provides additional arguments, or facts, in order to put their case to maximum advantage.

Positive Indicators	Negative Indicators
Seeks to understand the other parties' positions through questioning, listening and summarizing. Presents facts in support of arguments. Carries out research in and around the situation. Highlights discrepancies and inconsistencies in the arguments of others.	Undertakes little preparation. Quick to reveal own position. Fails to consider, identify and exploit the weaknesses in the arguments of others. Does not assert own views in discussions.

Development Thought-provokers	
Activist	Place yourself 'in the shoes' of the person you will be negotiating with. Think about what they want to achieve, the resources they have and so on.
Reflector	When you last negotiated, what did you do well, what did you do poorly and what can you do differently next time?
Theorist	Read *Impact and Influence*, by R. Hale and P.J. Whitlam, published by Kogan Page, 1999.
Pragmatist	Develop some tailor-made open questions that you can use for gaining information.

28 Tenacity

Stays with a position or plan of action until the desired objective is achieved or is no longer reasonable. Displays perseverance.

Positive Indicators	Negative Indicators
Maintains a view or a position over a protracted period.	Gives up when the going gets tough.
Uses opportunities to express and re-express that view.	Forget the view or idea; describes it as unimportant.
Uses different approaches, situations and arguments to express that view.	Fails to take opportunities to re-express the view or idea for fear of reprisals.
Links the view to other agendas.	Holds a view or aim but uses the same old approaches and arguments – fails to explore the views of others and adapt approach.
Explores how the held view may benefit different parties.	

	Development Thought-provokers
Activist	Take opportunities to express the desired outcome using the 'broken record' approach.
Reflector	Write down the objective you are trying to achieve; read it every morning.
Theorist	Read Steven Covey's *The Seven Habits of Highly Effective People*, published by Simon & Schuster, 1998, particularly habits 1 and 2.
Pragmatist	Plan how you can link your objective into the agenda of meetings you attend.

29 Independence

Takes actions in which the main influence is their own beliefs or principles, rather than being influenced by others.

Positive Indicators	Negative Indicators
Able to make decisions, make plans or take actions based largely on own appraisal of a situation.	Continually refers decisions to others.
	Lacks self-confidence.
Refers very little to others – perhaps only in exceptional circumstances.	Demonstrates greater faith in the judgement of others than in own.
Will take an unpopular stand if it fits with broad organizational direction and values.	Displays a tendency to follow rather than lead.
Confident in own abilities and judgement.	

Development Thought-provokers	
Activist	Make that decision you have been pondering over.
Reflector	Identify the anticipated outcomes of a decision, on your own.
Theorist	List the factors that are stopping you making a decision.
Pragmatist	Commit to making one significant decision a day or week.

30   Teamwork

Able to work cooperatively as a member of a diverse team and be committed to the overall team objective, rather than the achievement of own interests.

Positive Indicators	Negative Indicators
Knows strengths and weaknesses of team members. Seeks to include others when in a team. Works to prevent factions developing within teams. Encourages people to express their opinions. Supports and encourages team members.	Devalues the opinions of some. Listens only to a select group or individual. Avoids confrontation and differences of opinion within the group. Pays little attention to the group's dynamics, simply concentrating on the task to be achieved.

Development Thought-provokers	
Activist	Try changing your behaviour in the team – for example, be more supportive.
Reflector	Ask your team members about how you contribute to the team.
Theorist	Read J.R. Katzenbach and D.K. Smith's *The Wisdom of Teams*, published by HBS Press, 1998.
Pragmatist	List the team's goals, list out your own goals, and plan how you can work harder on the areas of discrepancy.

31 Compliance

Keeps to company policy and/or procedures. Seeks approval from the correct authority for making changes.

Positive Indicators	Negative Indicators
Aware of company policies and procedures in relation to all role-related issues. Holds the view that procedures and policies exist in order to protect individuals and the organization. Has never taken critical actions without reference to the organization's existing policy and procedural framework. Able to articulate the limits of own responsibility.	Unaware of the existence of the policies that should guide actions. Regularly ignores those policies and places organization, self and team members at risk. Will rarely ask for guidance or advice preferring to 'guess' what should be done.

Development Thought-provokers	
Activist	Meet and talk with 'specialists' about the existing policy and procedure frameworks within the organization.
Reflector	Consider how your following, or otherwise, of a procedure contributed to achieving a task.
Theorist	Read the procedure/policy manuals.
Pragmatist	Plan how you might implement an organizational procedure to a hypothetical or historical situation.

32 Acceptability

Personal style not likely to be abrasive or irritating to colleagues or customers/ clients. Not likely to alienate others.

Positive Indicators	Negative Indicators
Self-aware; understands the impact of personal behaviour on others.	Comes across as patronizing or smarmy.
Seeks to genuinely involve others.	Forces opinions 'down the throats of others'.
Listens and questions in order to understand.	Seems to hold an 'I am right' opinion all the time.
Gives people time to come to their own conclusions.	Displays a defensive reaction when people criticize or offer ideas.
Respects the opinions of others.	Never seeks the opinions of others.

Development Thought-provokers	
Activist	Ask more open questions.
Reflector	Think about those who you get on with. What do you do to get on with them?
Theorist	Read Steven Covey's *The Habits of Highly Effective People*, published by Simon & Schuster, 1998, particularly habits 4, 5 and 6.
Pragmatist	Write a personal aim based on the positive and negative ideas given above.

33   Assertiveness

Able to confront others by saying what they want, think, need and feel but not at the expense of the other person. Seeks win–win. Able to say 'no' without causing offence or feeling guilty.

Positive Indicators	Negative Indicators
Describes what is thought, felt and desired.	Ignores the feelings and desires of others.
Expresses views fully when questioned; holds no manipulative hidden agenda.	Withholds own opinions and feelings; unable to express own point of view.
Seeks to develop win–win relationships with all.	Willing to let others win whilst personally losing out.
Respects the opinions of others and seeks to hear those opinions.	Tries to create a scapegoat in many situations.

Development Thought-provokers	
Activist	Listen to others before saying what you think, feel and desire, then work on a mutually agreeable solution.
Reflector	Think about occasions when you were passive or occasions when you were aggressive. How can you be more assertive?
Theorist	Read books on assertiveness.
Pragmatist	Plan how you will be more assertive with someone you work with.

34   Resilience

Handles disappointment and/or rejection whilst maintaining effectiveness in role.

Positive Indicators	Negative Indicators
Able to put setback into perspective. Reflects on rejection and disappointment, trying to identify lessons learnt. Holds a mindset that suggests that mistakes and disappointments can strengthen. Seeks the views of others.	Sees disappointments and setbacks as complete losses. Unable to put issues into perspective and plan for a new future. Sees setbacks as personal failure; adopts a 'victim' mentality. Rarely receives feedback because of the debilitating effect it has.

Development Thought-provokers	
Activist	Talk to others about what went wrong and why it went wrong.
Reflector	Think about your last setback. Evaluate its 'real' importance to you.
Theorist	Think about your situation, think about what you want to achieve and develop your personal vision.
Pragmatist	Think about your last setback, identify the lesson learnt from it and then plan what you are going to do next.

35   Change orientation

Willing to embrace and welcome change, rather than take a stance of active or passive resistance. Consistently seeks new ways of doing things.

Positive Indicators	Negative Indicators
Always exploring new ways of working. Always comparing organizational practice with practices elsewhere. Encourages others to identify new ways of working. Tries to do him/herself out of a job. Holds a mindset along the lines of 'there will always be a role for someone who continually seeks to improve'.	Adheres rigidly to existing practice. Voices opinions like, 'We have tried that before', 'Why change it?' and 'Let's wait and see what happens'. Does not encourage or use the ideas of team members.

Development Thought-provokers	
Activist	Always ask the question, of self and others, 'How can I improve?'.
Reflector	Think about your past reactions to change. How would you like to react to change in the future?
Theorist	Read R.G. Chang's *Mastering Change Management*, published by Kogan Page, 1995.
Pragmatist	Visit other organizations and think about how you can develop their ideas within yours.

36   Problem analysis

Identifies problems, finding relevant information, relating data from different sources and identifying possible causes of problems.

Positive Indicators	Negative Indicators
Knows who, when and where to get information from. Able to assemble component views in order to develop a robust perspective. Able to identify the contributing factors in a given situation. Can assess the relative importance and influence of component parts of a situation.	Has poor information networks. Has poor questioning and listening skills. Unable to understand individual motives for describing a given situation in a given way. Unable to apply a systems thinking approach to a situation.

Development Thought-provokers	
Activist	Make a list of who you know and what information they can provide you with.
Reflector	Identify how and from where you got information for a previous key decision. With hindsight, what information would you have liked and where could you have got it?
Theorist	Read R. Hale and P.J. Whitlam's *Practical Problem Solving and Decision Making*, published by Kogan Page, 1997.
Pragmatist	Plan a series of meetings with 'information holders'.

37   Verbal fact-finding

Gathers information for decision-making through the effective use of questioning.

Positive Indicators	Negative Indicators
Uses open questions in order to explore the real meaning in messages. Summarizes comment in order to develop a robust understanding. Probes with sensitivity and empathy. Looks for conflicting opinions in order to test ideas.	Makes assumptions; jumps to conclusions. Accepting/uncritical of information given. Body languages conveys disinterest in messages. Fails to use silence to encourage people to give more information.

Development Thought-provokers	
Activist	Ask more open questions and paraphrase the responses.
Reflector	Ask for feedback, and think about the messages you might be conveying through your body language.
Theorist	Read *Impact and Influence*, by R. Hale and P.J. Whitlam, published by Kogan Page, 1999.
Pragmatist	Plan for the next questioning situation. Think about how you can really understand the message being conveyed.

38   Innovativeness

Creates and implements new commercial insights and the management of others. Generates and/or recognizes imaginative, creative solutions in work–related situations and opportunities.

Positive Indicators	Negative Indicators
Holds two or three ideas about how things could be done differently. Has introduced new systems and approaches. Demonstrates 'off–beat' ideas, lateral 'outside the box' thinking. Is very willing to try out concepts/ideas and pragmatically develop them in own environment.	Seeks compliance within team. Has rigid ways of working. Promotes stability of processes and practices. Rarely expresses ideas. Rarely introduces change. Inclined to replicate practices of others.

Development Thought-provokers	
Activist	Ask your team to present ideas on how things can be done differently.
Reflector	Think about how things could be improved.
Theorist	Read O. Hussey, *The Innovation Challenge*, published by Wiley, 1997.
Pragmatist	Think about a current project, list five ways of achieving the same end.

39   Decisiveness

Ready to make decisions, render judgements, take action or commit oneself.

Positive Indicators	Negative Indicators
Makes judgements based on own experiences. Assesses the importance and need for any action. Holds a 's/he who waits is lost' mindset. Can see 'the wood for the trees' and takes action. Able to rapidly assess the prevailing circumstances.	Waits for more information. Ponders situations before taking any action, if any action is taken at all – analysis to paralysis. Often 'sits on the fence'. Makes poor assessments of prevailing influences on any given situation.

Development Thought-provokers	
Activist	Make that decision today.
Reflector	Consider the worst outcome and the best outcome arising from a decision.
Theorist	Read R. Hale and P.J. Whitlam's, *Practical Problem Solving and Decision Making*, published by Kogan Page, 1997.
Pragmatist	Weigh up the pros and cons today and make your decision now.

40 Environmental awareness

Aware of changing political, economic, social and technological environment likely to affect the job or the organization.

Positive Indicators	Negative Indicators
Has an idea of the impact of technology on future ways of working.	Has 'head in the sand' approach.
Relates the changing economic scene and forecasts to the development of the business.	Unaware of emerging trends in public opinion and preferences.
Can describe the impact of demographic trends on future demand.	Disinterested in, and dismissive of, contextual information.
Aware of the impact of impending legislation and emerging legislation.	

Development Thought-provokers	
Activist	Deliver a presentation on the trends affecting your organization over the next five years.
Reflector	Review journals that cover economics, social and legal trends.
Theorist	Subscribe to journals, such as the *Economist*.
Pragmatist	Set aside an afternoon a month for researching current trends and future influences on your organization.

41   Vision

Able to stand apart from day-to-day activities and see the whole, focusing on major strategic goals rather than tackling each issue as soon as it arises.

Positive Indicators	Negative Indicators
Has a desired end point in mind. Relates existing activities to attain that end point. Prioritizes work in relation to the desired position. Articulates how activities fit in the context of the long-term vision. Adapts that vision in light of shifting influences.	Has poorly developed view of the future shape of the business. Has ill-defined understanding of the contribution today's activities will make on tomorrow. Shifts focus of activity based on short-term influences. Has poor contextual understanding of the long-term issues (threats and opportunities) confronting the business.

Development Thought-provokers	
Activist	Create a list of the longer-term influences likely to affect your organization. Meet with individuals from within your organization to discuss these influences.
Reflector	Identify the factors that have influenced your organization over the last five years.
Theorist	Place the factors likely to influence your organization under the following headings – social, technological, environmental, political and legal. Give each of these a weighting – 5 for highest impact, 1 for lowest impact.
Pragmatist	Identify ways in which your organization should respond to the threats.

42   Organizational design

Able to determine and develop the most effective organization to accomplish a task.

Positive Indicators	Negative Indicators
Able to deconstruct a large goal into component tasks and roles.	Uses existing or old structures and designs when attempting to deliver.
Creates systems that facilitate the achievement of that goal.	Creates unnecessary bureaucracy in order to deliver the task.
Seeks to develop the interdynamics (culture) that will best achieve a given goal.	Does not build checks and balances into systems in order to measure effectiveness.
Able to recognize the technical and interpersonal skills required for the accomplishment of a task.	Unaware of the role of collectively held values and norms on the delivery.

Development Thought-provokers	
Activist	Think about who is doing what, when and why in your team. Identify where and how things can be improved.
Reflector	Observe your team at work, identify what skills they need to do their job and what knowledge they require.
Theorist	Develop a flow diagram which describes the processes and procedures within your team.
Pragmatist	Develop a plan which describes how work could be better organized within the team.

43   Planning and organization

Establishes a course of action for self and/or others to accomplish a specific goal; plans proper assignments of personnel and appropriate allocation of resources.

Positive Indicators	Negative Indicators
Breaks down the larger task into components for others to achieve. Prioritizes each of those components. Allocates individuals with appropriate abilities to deliver on the components. Briefs those individuals on what needs to be done by when.	Fails to describe how a team's or individual's role links to the achievement of the larger objective. Fails to resource an individual or team. Does not construct monitoring mechanisms.

Development Thought-provokers	
Activist	Working with a current goal, identify who is doing what and by when. Discuss progress to date and set new targets.
Reflector	Think about a complex goal you and your team achieved. How did you coordinate the component tasks of that goal? How could those components have been better coordinated?
Theorist	Read one of the many books on planning.
Pragmatist	Take a goal and develop a 'map' that describes how the component parts of the goal are interlinked.

44   Self-organization

Able to efficiently schedule own time and activities.

Positive Indicators	Negative Indicators
Knows what is important and works on it. Identifies what needs to be achieved by when. Delegates tasks to others. Consistently delivers the goods.	Confusion about priorities. Works on the principle of 'do what's on top of the pile'. Has many people chasing for completion of projects. Rarely says 'no'.

Development Thought-provokers	
Activist	Meet with your manager and, together, develop a list of your priorities.
Reflector	Record what you are spending your time doing in a diary. Review this diary. How do your activities relate to your priorities?
Theorist	Read books on managing your time.
Pragmatist	Set yourself 'milestones' when setting yourself a target. Review how you are doing against those 'milestones'.

45 Delegation

Utilizes subordinates effectively. Allocates decision-making and other responsibilities to the appropriate individuals.

Positive Indicators	Negative Indicators
Gives tasks to individuals who have the potential to deliver. Gives clear instructions about what needs to be done by when. Sets up review meetings. Makes self available for support and advice.	Does not describe the task clearly. Provides no ongoing support or advice. Supplies no clear timeframes. Gives little information on how the task fits into the wider context.

Development Thought-provokers	
Activist	Give a team member a task that they do not normally do, brief them on what you want, by when and provide ongoing support.
Reflector	What did you last delegate? How did you delegate? Was it successful? What could be improved about the way you delegated?
Theorist	Look at the way other people delegate what do they do well, what do they do badly and what are you going to do differently.
Pragmatist	Develop a checklist for effective delegation and use it when briefing team members – what the task is, when it needs to be done, how it should be presented and so on.

46   Management control

Establishes procedures to monitor and/or regulate processes, tasks or activities of subordinates, and job activities and responsibilities. Takes action to monitor the results of delegated assignments or projects.

Positive Indicators	Negative Indicators
Review meetings are seen as the norm by team members. Monitoring meetings are integrated into all projects regardless of size. Reviews lead to improvement ideas. Ideas generated through monitoring meetings are acted upon and themselves reviewed.	No targets are set. No timeframes are identified. Reviews lead to plans but no actions. Monitoring does little to enhance performance.

Development Thought-provokers	
Activist	Set up review meetings with team members. Describe and develop with them measures of success.
Reflector	Identify the monitoring mechanisms that are in place. How can they be enhanced?
Theorist	Read *Target Setting and Goal Achievement*, by R. Hale and P.J. Whitlam, published by Kogan Page, 1998.
Pragmatist	Identify how monitoring can be improved and develop a plan for introducing those new methods for monitoring.

47 Development of team members

Develops the skills and competencies of subordinates through training and development activities related to current and future jobs. This will include coaching as well as other on–job development techniques.

Positive Indicators	Negative Indicators
Uses methods for determining real development needs.	Fails to recognize that people learn in different ways.
Uses mistakes as learning opportunities.	Provides solutions too quickly, rather than letting people work it out for themselves.
Encourages people to share their learning.	Sees learning as attending courses.
Uses a variety of methods to support work-based learning.	

Development Thought-provokers	
Activist	Make debriefing – exploring what went well and what could be improved – a normal feature of meetings.
Reflector	Encourage team members to 'shadow' individuals in other parts of the organization, or indeed in other organizations.
Theorist	Read Peter Honey's *101 Ways to Develop Your People*, published by Peter Honey Publications, 1994.
Pragmatist	Describe your latest 'learning' to team members. Get them to do the same.

48   Customer and market focus

Able to understand internal and external customer requirements as a part of developing long-term customer satisfaction.

Positive Indicators	Negative Indicators
Can articulate existing customer expectations.	Receives poor satisfaction ratings from customers.
Able to describe trends in the competitors' performance.	Receives many complaints – many covering the same old issues.
Has mechanisms in place in order to understand evolving customer expectations.	Has no concept of mutuality between customers and providers.
Understands how the customer's business is evolving.	Has no forums for exploring expectations and issues.

Development Thought-provokers	
Activist	Visit customers. Discuss with them their expectations and changing requirements.
Reflector	Review the data generated by customer surveys.
Theorist	Read books such as Chang and Kelly's *Satisfying Internal Customers First*, published by Kogan Page, 1995.
Pragmatist	Develop a tool for surveying customer views and requirements.

49   Technological literacy

Able to make use of existing information technology necessary to expedite work and/or as may be necessary to communicate fast and effectively.

Positive Indicators	Negative Indicators
Able to use existing technology to send e-mail messages.	Unable to use existing technology to send e-mail messages.
Able to search for information on the Internet.	Unable to search for information on the Internet.
Able to organize tasks and diary using technology.	Unable to organize tasks and diary using technology.
Able to produce dynamic presentations using existing software.	Unable to produce dynamic presentations using existing software.

Development Thought-provokers	
Activist	Use the programmes and the help screens, make mistakes and have a go.
Reflector	Stop and think about why something is not working or is working – keep a notebook that records how you used the software.
Theorist	Read help manuals such as the *Windows for Dummies* series.
Pragmatist	Attend a course on using the software. Plan how you are going to use the knowledge gained.

50 Monitoring

Oriented to attend to, and skilled in accurately evaluating, the performance and effectiveness of others and projects through observation and review of documented activities.

Positive Indicators	Negative Indicators
Aware of the progress in projects.	Allows projects to slip behind schedule.
Knows the status of achievements against goals.	Not clear regarding the progress of a project against the plan.
Able to accurately estimate completion times on assignments.	Unaware of the contribution others are making to a task or assignment.

Development Thought-provokers	
Activist	Meet with project or team members and get a progress report from them against schedules/plans.
Reflector	Stop and think about how a project could be brought into line and encourage others to think through what they ought to do to ensure deadlines are met.
Theorist	Read about project planning and control, and look at the various tools and techniques available.
Pragmatist	Devise a monitoring and control system using or adapting a recognized tool (for example, a network or PERT chart).

Index